Teaching Key Stage 1 Music

A complete, step-by-step scheme of work
by Ann Bryant

International MUSIC Publications

Published 2002

Editor: Louisa Wallace
Music and text setting: Barnes Music Engraving Ltd.
CD: Michael Klein, Heartbeat Sound
Cover Design: Dominic Brookman
Illustrations for Contrast cards: Maggie Brand
Photography: Moose Azim

Contents

Foreword

To all those fellow Key Stage 1 teachers who fear and dread teaching music: You, like me, have probably never picked up a musical instrument since primary school, let alone can remember how to read music. So how do we teach it?

I have been teaching for two years, the latter as music co-ordinator! I had looked at various music schemes, but I found them all uninspiring, monotonous and complicated to understand. I began to question myself: am I teaching music progressively? Am I covering all National Curriculum objectives? Are the children enjoying it? Are they learning anything?

When I was first approached to trial Ann's book I was horrified. I felt incompetent. But to my amazement it works! I have been learning *with* the children, I can see the progression, and the scheme is definitely non-threatening. The children are continually interactive and thoroughly absorbed in what they are doing. Music lessons are fun! Most importantly, from a co-ordinator's point of view, I was confident that every aspect of the National Curriculum was being taught, and more! To my surprise, I even found myself being able to support my colleagues.

This is a scheme I would certainly recommend to any Key Stage 1 teacher, specialist or not.

Mel Bussell
Music Co-ordinator
Southgate Infants School
Alvaston
Derby

Ann Bryant has produced a unique course for Key Stage 1 Music. It really does give so-called 'non-specialists' a superb course in teaching Key Stage 1 but it is unique because music specialists will find so much in this course which will enhance – or perhaps transform – their teaching.

As a traditionally trained 'music specialist', I first encountered Ann's work at a music conference and subsequently used so many of her musical ideas and games for infants that it revolutionised my teaching. Our Year 2 children are now achieving levels of musicianship which are regarded in the area as quite exceptional.

Ann's approach is to so involve children in music, movement and games that they cannot fail to appreciate pitch, rhythm and pulse. She chooses music for listening exercises with great intuitive feel for what the children will appreciate. By using her excellent notes, non-musicians will feel very comfortable leading their children to a real appreciation of music. Using those methods, all children can achieve and all teachers can provide an excellent music course.

So many courses try to give non-musicians an entry into music teaching – they provide sub-standard musical examples, music which is totally inappropriate for the children's voices at this age or expect some piano playing. As a music specialist and a pianist, I hardly ever play the piano for Key Stage 1 children. I mostly sing unaccompanied and very occasionally play the guitar. This course gives non-musicians permission to do the same!

For the non-musicians who have to take on Key Stage 1 music teaching – go for this course. Do not be frightened – it will provide all you need and your children will have a superb musical training. Can't play the piano? Good! The piano is the last thing Key Stage 1 children need to appreciate music. Just use Ann Bryant's lesson plans.

For the music specialist – this course will give you so many ideas for wonderful interactive games which will so enhance what you offer that I guarantee that your music teaching will never be the same again! By taking the best of Kodály solfège training and Dalcroze musicianship together with the imagination of an inspired and experienced teacher, Ann Bryant is giving everyone who uses this course the very best way to introduce young children to the joys of music.

Helen Mackinnon MA, LRAM, LTCL
Director of Music
Berkhampstead School
Music Department
Pittville Circus Road
Cheltenham
Gloucester

Acknowledgements

My grateful thanks to Carol Grey and Helen Mackinnon for their help, and especially to Mel Bussell for her invaluable support throughout the preparation of this book.

Thanks too, to Louisa Wallace, my lovely editor, for her unstinting hard work and fantastic contribution to the making of the book.

I'd also like to say a big 'Thank you' to Ros Simmonds for her wonderful support and very kind words.

And finally, most of all, my thanks and much love to Caroline Salmon, who has given me unfailing support and encouragement in my work over the years, as well as a platform on which to display it.

Thanks to the following who took part in the recording:

Bedgebury Junior School, Kent
Carol Gray, Year 2 choir

Dulwich Prep School, Cranbrook, Kent
Class 1G, Class 1P and Reception L.R.
Lauren Pattle (solo *The Dingleden Train*)
Leo White, John Gabriel, Katie Willets, Sophie Griggs and Tom Harvey (solos *I'm Fred Wheelie Bin*)
Sebastien Cottle (solo *What's My Name?*)
Hannah Pilkington, Lucy Baxter and Holly Pilkington (*What Annie McCrae Wanted For Tea*)
Claire Masterton, Year 3 choir (*The Giant's Garden*)

Introduction

Welcome generalists! This scheme of work has been written with you in mind and is deliberately non-threatening. By the time you've done one lesson, you'll feel more confident and secure about your ability to teach music. By the time you've done several, you'll feel that the misty world of music has become clear and bright! This scheme is easy to follow lesson by lesson. Every lesson is action-based and designed to be a lot of fun for all involved.

Non-musicians can teach music very effectively. I know you may have only spent half a term learning about the teaching of music at your training college, and I bet you've forgotten most of that! It doesn't matter. I'm assuming you know nothing. It also doesn't matter if you can't read music. In fact it's better not to, unless you can do it easily. I've often seen teachers glued to music, struggling to read it, and unaware that they are sacrificing the all-important contact with their class.

One of the biggest worries for generalists is feeling that you don't have the facility to assess whether or not your lesson has been a success. In this book *you* learn as the children learn, and the point of the activity is always clear, so that the course makes sense to you, and your teaching takes shape. This, in turn, gives you the confidence to assess. You won't be blindly following instructions and hoping that you're 'doing it right'! You won't just be making a token gesture towards fulfilling the National Curriculum. Instead, you will be taking charge of your music teaching.

This course is not just a lot of isolated ideas, it is progressive. Each skill is learnt, developed, reinforced and integrated into the rest of the learning, so that you will truly see yourself and the children becoming more and more musical. This reinforcement and revision forms an essential part of a child's musical education.

No need to read music

The CD included with this book precludes the necessity to read music. The songs are written out in case you want to play them, but the CD is a useful tool when learning and rehearsing a new song because each song is sung through first, then repeated with just the accompaniment for you and your class to sing along to. That way it gives you an idea of how each song sounds. The CD was recorded live, in a classroom environment and so it is realistic! We have used various combinations of voices on the recording

(such as solos, duets, adult voices, etc.) and have added some basic percussion here and there, merely to vary the sound and add to the texture. You can arrange the songs as you wish.

Once the songs are learnt, it really is best to work without the CD, as this will encourage much more participation from the children and allow you to go at your own pace. The songs are located at the back of the book with page references so you can find them easily for use in any future lessons. There are also photocopiable lyric sheets for optional use when learning the Year 2 songs. You may want to introduce other songs as well as those used in the course. The CD also offers help with many of the musical activities, providing examples of rhythm sequences and so on.

National Curriculum requirements

This book is totally attuned to the National Curriculum (England) and much of the work covered will fulfil the requirements of the National Guidelines for Scottish Levels A–B. Listening and applying knowledge are developed through the interrelated skills of performing, composing and appraising. The lessons here use a range of musical activities that integrate these skills. Children are required to work as a class and in smaller groups. In an ideal world more time would be allocated to learning music, however you may well find that you can use some of the songs or activities in the book at odd times of day if you have a few minutes to fill. The more these skills are developed, the greater the knock-on effect will be.

Remember, you may well find yourself learning alongside the children, which will strengthen the value of the whole learning process because you can ask the children, for example, if they think Jamie was walking in time with the music at that point. You might not be sure yourself. It will make you all consider the question carefully. This considering process is all part of listening and appraising.

Each term there is one piece of classical music to listen to. The pieces have been chosen carefully as 'attention grabbers', inspiring children to want to hear more classical music. Each piece is also a suitable length to avoid the risk of boredom. There are five pieces of classical music covered in the entire course. All are easy to obtain from any shop and it doesn't matter which recording you choose. The shop should advise you on price and availability.

Why teach music anyway?

Some children will go on to learn an instrument such as the piano or the violin. Good classroom music education is the perfect preparation for this. Most children, however, will not go on to learn an instrument but they will *all* benefit from having the added dimension of music in their lives. Music gives so much pleasure, whether you are listening to live or recorded music of whatever type, singing in a choir or group, playing in a band, or just dancing at a party. The skills you can develop from learning about music in these early years of Key Stage 1, particularly a sense of rhythm and the ability to read proper music notation, will prove invaluable later on in life. The ability to listen, to concentrate and to be aware lies at the heart of the music learning process. These are life skills, so the impact on other areas of the National Curriculum is enormous. At the core of the music learning process lies the ability to listen and discriminate aurally. You will see that this is the emphasis right from the very first lesson.

Music is a language. When a language is taught, the main aim is for the pupils to achieve communication in that language. With science the teacher tries to cultivate in the pupils a definite mental approach to the subject – a rationalisation and a conclusion about all experiments. Maths and English are now known as numeracy and literacy because it is these skills which are being developed. In the same way, music education should develop *listening* skills, with rhythmic and pitch senses at the core of the subject. Singing a song every so often, or listening to a piece of music and discussing it, are all *part of* the process, but you can liken them to having a list of ten French words to learn for homework – although it is a valuable part of learning the language, you can't rely on it to completely do the job. The aim is to *immerse* the children in music. For young children, absorbing musical language should be as painless as verbal language. So, many of the activities used here at the beginning of Year 1 are repeated, developed, deepened and extended throughout the course.

Action-based lessons

Music is often viewed as a very demanding subject for those learning and teaching it. As a result, many teachers choose to conduct their lessons in a very static way with children sitting down singing for the entire duration of the class. In music lessons, we are asking children to look, listen, concentrate, anticipate and be aware, sometimes within a rhythmic framework, and often while playing an instrument. Taking an active approach to lessons increases the ability to learn how to do all of this as it creates variety, relieves boredom and maintains concentration.

The National Curriculum recognises the importance of movement because the children can actually *feel* the style, mood, pulse, beat and rhythm of the music. The process becomes multi-sensory – and let's face it, it's much more fun moving about than sitting still! My training at music college involved a great deal of Dalcroze eurythmics, and I subsequently did a Dalcroze diploma. Dalcroze's entire philosophy involved the use of movement as a means of learning music, so rhythmic skills are developed at a deeper level. I have adapted many Dalcroze ideas (almost beyond recognition at times!) to devise this course of work for Key Stage 1.

If you have the use of a hall for your lessons, this is ideal. Otherwise move tables and chairs to clear a good space in the classroom. (I work in a hall where I'm lucky enough to be able to use coloured sticky tape on the floor to divide the hall area into four, square sections. I find it really useful to be able to refer to 'the red square', 'the green square', etc.)

Children should get into the habit of taking off socks and shoes, unless you are working on a carpet, for the simple reason that when they are all moving around their shoes will make too much noise on the floor. The skill of listening deserves great respect. Aural discrimination will only develop where you work with a background of silence.

Do I have to do exactly 12 lessons per term?

No. Nor do you have to make your lesson content exactly match what is set out in the book. It is inevitable that some activities will take more or less time than I have allowed. If you run out of time, simply start the next lesson at the point where you left off. If, however, you find there is not enough material in a particular lesson, go on to the following lesson. It doesn't matter if you get ahead because as you cover more concepts you will find more and more activities and songs that you want to revisit, either as reinforcement or simply because the children enjoyed them. There is also consolidation material built into every lesson, which gives you flexibility in your teaching. Remember this consolidation work is invaluable.

Do I have to cover all the Year 1 work before embarking on the Year 2 work?

The answer is yes. If you are starting this book with Year 2 children, begin by teaching them the Year 1 syllabus. You will find that you move much more quickly because the children are that bit older. Even though you probably won't be able to complete the Year 2 work by the end of Year 2, you will have delivered a very good scheme of work that meets the criteria of the National Curriculum (England).

Planning

Long-term planning

There are twelve 30-minute lessons per term for each year group. The pages for each year group have a marked edge for quick location. As I said right at the start, this course aims to teach *you* to teach the children, and for this reason the lesson plans become shorter as they go on – there becomes less of a need for explanation as you take more ideas on board. Don't be alarmed by this, it really is easy to follow. The more you take the time to lay the foundations thoroughly, the more enjoyable and natural your teaching will become.

Medium-term planning

Sorting out medium-term plans is made easier with manageable, achievable objectives. At the beginning of each term you will see the following text box:

> **Theme:** e.g. Contrasts. (You might like to develop this theme across the curriculum)
>
> **Concept:** e.g. Contrasting musical elements
>
> **Medium-term objective:** e.g. To understand the importance of listening to music, focusing on these contrasts: Loud/Quiet, High/Low, Smooth/Jumpy, Fast/Slow
>
> **Music to listen to:** e.g. *Carnival of the Animals* by Saint-Saëns
>
> **Songs:** The number of songs taught during the term (approx. 4 or 5)
>
> **Resources:** A list of the resources you will need throughout the term, e.g. a range of percussion instruments

Short-term planning

At the beginning of every lesson you will see the following headings:

Objective:

e.g. For Lesson 1, the objective is:

■ to recognise, respond to, create and evaluate the contrasts: Loud/Quiet

Additional resource: This will only appear if something specific is needed for this particular lesson, which is not listed in the main resources section at the beginning of the term

Occasionally you will see this sign *** against an activity. It means that the activity about to be covered here is tricky and may need a bit of extra preparation from you.

What else will I find in this book?

• Photographs to show how to hold and play various percussion instruments.

• A list of all the games and activities used in this scheme, where they were first taught and where, if anywhere, they were subsequently extended. This allows you to dip into a pool of reinforcement material whenever you want. If you've forgotten how to do a particular activity simply look back to the lesson where it was taught. Sometimes I suggest alternative starting or finishing ideas, but do always feel that you can also pick one of your own from the list at the back. You might want to choose something that you know works particularly well with your class, or something that you are aware is a weak area and could do with a little more work. Remember you can do any of the activities at odd times of the day if you have a spare five minutes! I cannot stress enough the value of revision, reinforcement and consolidation in music education.

• The Key Stage 1 Music National Curriculum (England) – at the back of the book for quick reference.

• Photocopiables: A recommended sample assessment grid that will allow you to keep a continuous assessment of your children with the minimum amount of paper work.

• Photocopiable templates for the **contrasts** and **note value cards**. (It will be clearly explained what these are as you come to need them.)

• Photocopiable song sheets for the Year 2 songs.

All you need to know – a quick revision of the National Curriculum!

1. What is PULSE?

Start clapping now… Make sure your claps are evenly spaced. You have created a pulse. Clap more slowly, but still with regular time spaces between each clap. Now you are clapping to a slower pulse. Then try clapping to a quicker pulse. A pulse is simply that!

2. What is a BEAT?

Each one of those evenly spaced claps you've just done is a beat. You can also say, 'Keep to the beat' which is another way of saying, 'Keep to the pulse' (just to confuse you!)

3. What is TEMPO?

Tempo is the speed at which you are playing or

singing. You can play or sing at a slower or faster tempo.

4. What is METRE?

Choose any speed and start clapping evenly again. Now keep clapping at the same speed, but count 1, 2, 3 repeatedly as you clap and make all the number 1s louder than the 2s and 3s. Now you have a metre. You are clapping in 3-time. Change your counting to go up to 4 each time, and make sure the 1s are louder than the 2s, 3s and 4s. Now you are clapping in 4-time. This is the most commonly-used metre and so is often called Common Time. Much of the work covered in this book will be in 4-time. You will have often heard the expression, 'Keep in time'. It means keep on the beat or keep a steady pulse as you play or sing. Remember that your pupils won't know what you mean when you first use this expression!

5. What is RHYTHM?

Clap *Happy Birthday to You*. You are doing more than just clapping a pulse or even a metre. You are arranging claps of different speeds into a pattern. This pattern is a rhythm. In another sense you can also say, 'She's got good rhythm' which means she clearly *feels* the pulse, the beat, the metre, the general flow of the music and is interpreting it accurately.

6. What is PITCH?

Sing *Happy Birthday to You*. You are singing higher and lower notes – i.e. notes of different pitch. This particular pattern of pitched notes combined with the rhythmic pattern is the composition for the song *Happy Birthday to You*.

7. What is TIMBRE?

Timbre simply means the quality of a musical sound. Claves have a wooden clacking timbre, drums a thuddy, deeper timbre and bells a high tinkling timbre etc.

8. What are DYNAMICS?

Dynamics is simply the musical term for how loudly or quietly you sing or play.

Using percussion instruments

You will need a variety of percussion instruments. We can divide percussion instruments into two categories – pitched and non-pitched.

- **Pitched** simply means that the instrument can produce different notes – like a xylophone or a glockenspiel. They can go up and down, making higher and lower notes.
- **Non-pitched** percussion instruments are those which cannot make higher and lower notes, like a drum, a tambourine or a shaker. You can simply play a pulse, a beat and a rhythm on these instruments.

You only need one pitched instrument – either a xylophone or a glockenspiel for you to play. You need enough non-pitched instruments for each child in the class, but some of these can be home made. Many of the activities involve the use of four different *contrasting* blocks of sound – four different types of instrument – such as tambourines, wood blocks, finger cymbals and maracas.

In a class of 24 children, you should ideally have the following:

- **6 tambourines**
- **6 tambours with beaters:** Tambours is the proper name for the drums which look like tambourines but without bells.
- **6 maracas or shakers:** These could be made from empty yoghurt pots, or a similar container, filled a centimetre, at the most, deep with dry rice or dry pasta. Best of all are empty Pringles containers!
- **6 wooden instruments:** Either claves, which are just two cylindrical sticks which can be tapped together or a simple wood block, which is a block of wood tapped with a wooden beater. You can create a similar sounding wooden instrument with something as simple as two wooden spoons or spatulas tapped against each other.
- **6 finger cymbals:** These are much easier to handle than triangles or Indian bells. They are different from the other instruments listed here because the sound they make when struck rings on, so they can produce a long note. However they are not effective for playing short notes because their sound is loud and glaring, drowning out any other sounds. Larger cymbals can also be used to great effect. Use just one cymbal, holding it by the handle and hitting it with a beater. This helps keep it under control. Children instinctively tend to rest the cymbal on their laps. This is fine when they are resting, but try to encourage them to hold it away from them slightly when they are playing, so that the sound can ring on.

The following show the best way to hold and play a selection of percussion instruments, taking into consideration that this is Key Stage 1.

Tambourine: Tap with curved fingers.

Shaker: For a controlled sound, tap one shaker into the palm of the hand.

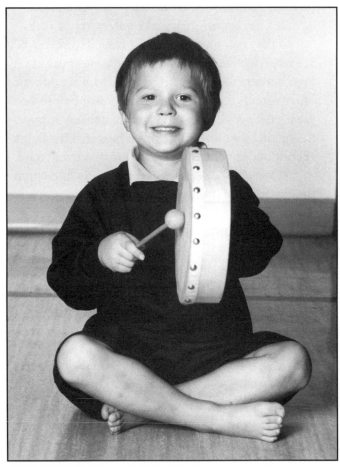

Tambour

Claves

Finger Cymbals: An up and down action is easiest.

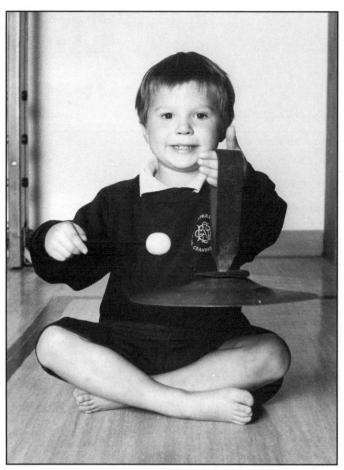

Cymbal: Hold cymbal away from the body to allow it to resonate.

Chapter 1
Year 1, Term 1

Theme: Contrasts

Concept: Contrasting musical elements

Medium-term objective:

■ To understand the importance of listening within music, with the focus on the contrasts: Loud/Quiet, High/Low, Smooth/Jumpy, Fast/Slow

Music to listen to: *Carnival of the Animals* by Saint-Saëns

Songs: *The Grand Old Duke Of York*; *Hickory Dickory Dock*; *Jump!*; *It's Me!*; *The Dingleden Train* and your own choice of songs, if required.

Resources: CD; a large selection of percussion instruments including a xylophone (see section at the end of the Introduction listing percussion instruments); 4 copies of each of the 8 contrasts cards from the back of the book; CD of *Carnival of the Animals*.

Lesson 1

Objective:

■ To recognise, respond to, create and evaluate the contrasts: Loud/Quiet

Additional resource: A cuddly toy

Loud/Quiet Activity 1

- Take off socks and shoes (this is something you should always ask the children to do).
- Have the children clustered around you and introduce Pepsi (any cuddly toy). Say that he likes to sleep on his tummy. Encourage a conspiratorial silence and put him in the middle of the floor.
- Whisper to the children that you're all going to stand up and creep around him very, very quietly. After a few seconds suggest to the children that you be naughty and wake up Pepsi with 3 loud claps. Do that. Pepsi is not impressed so put him back to sleep and repeat the creeping. Then wake him again, this time with 3 loud stamps. Now he really has had enough! Put him somewhere else to sleep. He has done his job. The children have already appreciated the difference between loud and quiet.

Loud/Quiet Activity 2

- Tap quietly at a steady pulse on any percussion instrument and encourage the children to tiptoe

around the room, keeping in time with the beat. Point out members of the class who are matching your beat well and encourage them to demonstrate for the others.

- Now try again, only this time, the children should stand still as soon as they hear you stop playing.
- Now for a CONTRAST. Explain to the children that a contrast is something completely different. Ask them to march around the room to your beat lifting up their knees and swinging their arms like soldiers. Play your steady beat loudly. Make sure no one moves before you start playing. Who's the best starter and who's the best stopper? Start and finish with a salute!
- Next choose whether you are going to play quietly or loudly and start playing. The children must listen carefully to see if you're playing the quiet creeping music or the loud marching music, and then move accordingly. The children are already learning to listen and discriminate.

Loud/Quiet Activity 3

- Divide the class into two teams, half at one side of the room as soldiers, and the other half at the other side as creepers. They must remember what they are. When they hear you playing the music (a loud or quiet beat), they must march or tiptoe around the room accordingly. The moment you change the music to the other team's music, they must stop and go quietly back to their starting place.

- Choose a contrasting instrument and agree on a sound signal that you will play when you want the children to swap places (i.e. the soldiers become creepers and vice versa). This signal could be any interesting sound that stands out. Repeat the game and incorporate this 'swap' signal once or twice.

At any point in this or future lessons, try to find examples of children who are matching either the beat, the character of the music, or both, particularly well; or those who are coping well with starting and stopping at exactly the right moment, and ask them to demonstrate.

Tapping names on the drum

- All sit in a circle. Tap your own name on the drum, emphasising the number of syllables. For example, 'Miss Buss-ell. My name has got 3 sounds. Let's see how many sounds there are in Be-cky's name.' Let each child tap their own name on the drum, trying to match the taps to the correct number of syllables.

Singing: A loud song and a quiet song

- Sing *The Grand Old Duke Of York* unaccompanied. Although a well-known nursery rhyme, the song is written out at the back of the book for your use if required (p.65). Sing loudly while marching and reinforcing the words with appropriate actions. Finish with a salute.
- Cluster together and sit down. Hum the tune of the nursery rhyme *Hickory Dickory Dock*. Do the children recognise it? Now sing it quietly.

Lesson 2

Objective:

■ As Lesson 1, incorporating the contrast: High/Low

Quiet and loud game

- Repeat the game of **soldiers** and **creepers** using your agreed swap signal, to recall and revise the contrast Loud/Quiet.

New contrast: High/Low

- Tap or slide your beater over a few of the high (top) notes on your xylophone. Ask the children to spread their 'wings' and 'fly' on tiptoe around the room. (It is impossible to consider High and Low without the implication of other musical elements. Your 'bird' music will inevitably also be quiet and quick. At

this stage the objective is to focus on the contrast, High/Low. But later you will see how the children are expected to discriminate in more detail.)

- Now for the contrast! Play the low notes at the bottom of the xylophone and ask the children to walk slowly and heavily like an elephant. Stepping *this* slowly is a particular challenge to children. Ask any child who is matching the music with their movements very well, to demonstrate to the others. (Again, it is impossible to consider the musical element Low in isolation, but this is where the focus lies.)

Contrasts

- To play this game, you need to divide the class into four groups:

  soldiers
  creepers
  birds
  elephants

- Place each group in four corners of the room. Next revise your swap signal. You are going to play the music for the four different contrasts which each group represents. When you play the elephant music for example, that group should move around the room like elephants, stopping and returning to their corner only when the music changes. Continue in any order and when all four groups have had a turn, play your swap signal. When they hear this signal the children should quietly walk in a clockwise direction to the next corner. Ask them what they represent. Repeat the game as often as you want with the children in a new persona each time.

Tapping names on the drum

- Repeat this activity from Lesson 1.

Signals

- This new activity will become a regular listening exercise to open the lesson.
- The children are sitting in a space of their own. Show the children how your xylophone is 'magic'. Play a high C and an even higher G at the top of the xylophone whilst saying 'Stand up!' The children should stand. Now play at the bottom of the xylophone, a G followed by the C below it. The children will probably sit down instinctively. So you can say the xylophone is magic because *you* didn't tell them to sit down – they did it automatically! Repeat these two signals – **stand up** and **sit down** – a few times. Look for children who are focusing on listening rather than looking at your hands and are quick to react to the change.

Singing

- If time, finish with one of the songs from Lesson 1.

Lesson 3

Objectives:

- To consolidate the contrasts: Loud/Quiet, High/Low
- To introduce the contrast: Smooth/Jumpy

Additional resource: A CD or tape of your choice

Contrasts

- Start the lesson with this game from Lesson 2. Revise the concepts Loud/Quiet and High/Low with this game.

Pass the contrasts cards

- This is more of a static game to revise contrasts.
- Sit in a circle. Using music from a CD or tape of your choice, pass the cards, **soldier** (loud) and **creeper** (quiet) around the circle while the music is playing. When the music stops, the person holding the **soldier** card should say their name in a loud voice. The person holding the **creeper** card should whisper their name. Continue like this. Other skills here are awareness and anticipation – making sure that when you've passed on your card, you're aware of the other card coming round next!
- Now try this game with the **bird** (high) card and the **elephant** (low) card. The children holding the cards when the music stops must say their names in a high or low voice, according to the card they have. Some children may confuse high with loud *or* quiet and others may be self-conscious. Don't worry, this game is good for developing performance skills and self-confidence.
- Try the game using all four **contrasts cards**!

Signals

- Revise the **signals game** from Lesson 2 ('Stand Up, Sit Down'). Add a new signal – **clap 3 times**. For this one, choose a note in the middle of the xylophone and play it 3 times. (Stick to the same note each time you play the game.) The children should wait until they have heard all 3 notes and then clap 3 times at the same speed.

New contrast: Smooth/Jumpy

- Talk about a snake sliding smoothly along without any bumps, then all try the action of a snake by walking very smoothly, with your two hands together, palms touching and fingers leading the

way, being the snake's head. See if the children can tell you why it doesn't work if they try to slide along on the floor. (They haven't got snakes' bodies so they can't go smoothly!) Slide the beater around anywhere on the xylophone for the snake music.

- The opposite of Smooth is Jumpy – like a frog. To create suitable frog music, play a drum in the following way: 1 loud beat, followed by 3 quiet ones repeated continually. The children should only do a frog jump on the loud beat and then wait during the 3 quiet beats for the next jump. This requires concentrated listening. Keep reminding the children about this, and choose a good demonstrator to show the others. Those watching could clap on the strong (loud) beat only.

Singing: *Jump!* (music: p.66)

- With the help of the CD, tracks 1 and 2, learn the song *Jump!* which has plenty of bounce and so fits with our concept of Jumpy. (You may want to learn the song yourself beforehand and teach it to the children without the use of the CD or you may want to make use of the pause button to sing and copy!) Track 1 is with the vocal line, track 2 is just the accompaniment. Follow the actions as they appear in the song. On the words, 'step it in a square', make the shape of a square with your feet by taking 2 steps forward and 2 steps back.

Jump!

Get ready now, 'cause we're all going to *pow!*
Go *pow! pow!*
Clap to the beat
And you step it in a square.
Yes, it's really neat,
So now you jump in the air.

2. click!
  3. stamp!
  4. shake!

Lesson 4

Objective:

- To consolidate the contrasts: Loud/Quiet; High/Low and Smooth/Jumpy

Signals

- Revise the three signals you have learnt so far by repeating them randomly several times. Try to encourage the children to listen independently rather than copy others. Add two new signals – **lie down** and **sit up**. **Lie down** is rather like **sit down** (G C), but here you need to fill in the notes between. So at the bottom of the xylophone, you play the notes G F E D C in quick succession. For **sit up** simply reverse these notes – C D E F G.

- Try playing an elimination game with the signals the children now know. Play the signals randomly and whoever gets it wrong is 'out'. If all the children keep getting the signals right then it is the last to respond who is 'out'.

Contrasts: incorporating Smooth/Jumpy

- Play a game of **contrasts**, this time with six teams of children responding to your randomly ordered music representing **loud** (soldiers), **quiet** (creepers), **high** (birds), **low** (elephants), **smooth** (snakes), and **jumpy** (frogs). Play the swap signal for the children to change places and repeat as often as you want.

Singing: *Jump!* (p.66)

- Finish by revising the song *Jump!*

Lesson 5

Objective:

- To learn to play and respect percussion instruments and the sound they make

Additional resource: A blindfold

An introduction to playing percussion instruments

- **Preparation:** Sit in a circle and put all the instruments in the middle. You'll need instruments with a variety of different sounds, and there must be at least two of each type. In a class of 24 children you might have:

  - 3 tambourines
  - 3 drums
  - 3 pairs of finger cymbals
  - 3 pairs of claves
  - 3 maracas (shakers)
  - 3 wood blocks
  - 3 triangles
  - 3 cymbals

- It is vital that the children understand the importance of sound and silence and that they learn to respect the instruments right from the word go. Explain that the instruments are precious and that any sound that comes from a musical instrument should be thought about and listened to. Twiddling the instrument is strictly not allowed! The following rhyme is useful when emphasising this rule:

> If you play before I say,
> You will find I take it away!

Ask the children to chant this important little poem with you. Every time you use instruments say the poem, and if anyone breaks the rule, take their instrument away for the next couple of activities. (I have always found that being ruthless in the early stages encourages good habits!)

- **Playing by copying:** Take one of every type of instrument and place the others, one in front of each child, at random. Next you should start to play an instrument of your choice. The children must watch carefully to see what you are playing. They should only join in if they have the same instrument in front of them. They should copy exactly what you play. Tell them that even when they've had one go, they might still get another later on. This keeps them concentrating.

Playing by copying

- Where possible play each instrument in more than one way. For example, play a tambourine first by shaking it, then by tapping it; shakers can be shaken continuously or intermittently; some wooden instruments can be scraped or tapped. Sometimes play fast, sometimes slowly, sometimes loudly and sometimes quietly. Talk about the wooden sounds, the ringing sounds, the *contrasting* ways in which you are playing. Play *even* beats (steady beats) if you think the children can copy you reasonably accurately, otherwise disregard the beat and concentrate on the technique. The photos in the Introduction show the correct holding and playing position of a selection of percussion instruments. Keep checking no one is twiddling his or her instrument. Try to breed sensitivity. Eye contact is good. Try being completely silent and still and see who can hear the clock ticking or other subtle sounds.

Singing: *It's Me!* (music: p.67)

- First learn the song, *It's Me!* The tune is that of the nursery rhyme, *Hickory Dickory Dock* but the words are different. You can use track 3 on the CD to help if you want.

It's Me!

Tiptoeing, tiptoeing round.
There's somebody stealing your sound!
Who can it be, who says 'It's me'?
The person who's stolen your sound.

- Next, clear away all the instruments except three that have contrasting sounds, for example, a pair of claves, a tambourine and a shaker. Put these in the middle of the circle. Make sure the children know the names of these three instruments and what they sound like. Now we're ready for the activity which goes with this song.
- Whilst singing the song *without* the CD, play the following game. One child sits in the middle with a blindfold on, near to the chosen instruments. Point to a child in the circle who should stand up and tiptoe around the child in the centre while you all sing the first two lines of the song. On the third line the tiptoeing child should 'steal' one of the instruments and go back to their place. At the end of the song that child says 'It's me!' Does the child in the centre recognise the voice? The child who has 'stolen' the instrument then plays it clearly, while the child in the centre tries to guess which instrument it is.

It's Me!

Lesson 6

Objective:

- To reinforce and extend the contrasts work

Additional resource: A blindfold

Signals

- Learn a new signal – **cross**. For this, play 2 quick loud taps on the drum. The children must put their hands on waists and wear a cross expression!
- Incorporate this new signal into an elimination game of **signals**.

Pass the contrasts cards: incorporating Smooth/Jumpy

- Play a game of **pass the contrasts cards** with the **snake** and **frog** cards. If anyone is holding the **snake** card when the music stops, they must say their name in a smooth voice. If someone is holding the **frog** card, they must say their name but separate the syllables as they say it. Learn the words which indicate Smooth and Jumpy in music. Smooth is called 'legato' and Jumpy is called 'staccato'.
- Next, play the game with these two cards and another pair of your choice.

Singing: *It's Me!* (p.67)

- Revise singing the song *It's Me!* and then play the game version. When you are playing this game, always sing unaccompanied. Change the instruments every two or three games. By having instruments which sound less obviously different from each other, such as tambourine, bells and tambour or even three shakers, the exercise in aural discrimination becomes slightly more difficult each time. If you use like instruments such as three shakers, take time before you start playing in order to discuss ways of identifying them, for example, 'the big green one'.
- If time, finish with *Jump!*

Lesson 7

Objective:

- To extend contrasts work with the focus on absorbing the contrasts of Loud/Quiet

Signals

- Add a new signal – **point to your eyes**. For this, choose a high note on the xylophone and tap it twice very gently. I usually say to the children, 'This is high, and there are two of them – just like your eyes!' Play the **signals game**, incorporating this new action. Try to get into the habit of starting the lesson with either a run-through of all the signals, in a different order each time, or an elimination game of **signals.**

Point to your eyes

A contrasts activity using instruments and action

- **Preparation:** Divide the class into four groups, one in each corner:
  1. instrumentalists playing *loudly* for the soldiers
  2. soldiers marching round
  3. instrumentalists playing *quietly* for the creepers
  4. creepers tiptoeing round

  Hand a percussion instrument to each child in groups one and three, and remind them of the poem from Lesson 5! Within each of these two groups try to have, if not exactly the same instrument, then instruments with the same type of sound. For example, you might have tambourines and tambours for group one and different types of wooden instruments for group three. This combination will give you two contrasting blocks of sound; the 'thuddy' sounds and the hollow, wooden sounds.

- **Instructions:** It is particularly important for the two instrumental groups to be looking at you at all times. When you point to group one they should play loudly. Play with them to help everyone keep to a steady marching beat. Group two (the soldiers) must march around in time to the music.

- When you point to group three, group one must instantly stop playing and group two (the soldiers) return to base. Now it is the turn of group three to play quietly, with your help, while group four (the creepers) tiptoe around the room.

- Remind the children of the swap signal before you

start and of how this tells them to move clockwise to the next corner, leaving their instruments behind. Arrange the four groups so children always move from an instrumental group to an action group and vice versa. You could tap a drum very gently when the children are moving around to the next place if you want.

Listening: *Carnival of the Animals* by Saint-Saëns – focusing on Loud/Quiet

- This popular piece of music is a great introduction to classical musical for children. Lots of animals are depicted musically in a series of short pieces as Saint-Saëns explores the sounds of different instruments. This music effectively covers the contrasts you have been learning about this term.

- Start with 'The March of the Lions'. You will hear a short introduction followed by a fanfare passage. Ask the children to stand up at this point and get ready to march round the room in time to the music. Listen out for the piano making the lion's roar. Ask the children to stand still and stretch out their 'claws' during these roars. Can they tell you how many roars there are?

- Now sit down to listen to 'The Cuckoo in the Woods'. This is a quiet calm piece. The woods are depicted by the piano and we hear 21 cuckoo calls on the clarinet. Before you play the music explain that the clarinet is an instrument that you have to blow, so it is a member of the wind family. Whilst listening, the children should lie down and close their eyes if they want. All count the cuckoo calls together very softly.

- If you can obtain a story of *Carnival of the Animals* or even any pictures of the animals portrayed in this piece, this visual aid will help to spark the children's imagination.

The more you can listen to these and future suggested extracts, the better. The music will then become more meaningful and the children will listen with heightened aural perception. Letting the music stimulate drawings or paintings also strengthens creativity and imagination. If you can find someone to give a short demonstration of any of the orchestral instruments, the children will be captivated. They love seeing the real thing, and hearing live music. At my school, we have regular visits from older children in the school who show the younger ones their instruments and play a piece or even just a few notes for them. This is also good for the confidence of the older child.

Singing: *It's Me!* (p.67)

- Try to stretch the children's aural listening skills further by using percussion instruments whose sounds are less contrasting still!

Lesson 8

Objective:

- To extend the contrasts work with the focus on absorbing the contrasting musical elements: Fast/Slow

Signals

- Play a game of this to start the lesson.

Listening: *Carnival of the Animals* – focusing on Fast/Slow

- Find the piece called 'Wild Asses'. The piano music is very fast. Choose a few children to gallop around the room to the music.
- Then play 'The Tortoise'. Encourage all the children to move very slowly. Notice that this tune is played on the cello which is the 'mummy' of the string family. Do you recognise the tune? If it were speeded up it would be the Can-Can. Most children will recognise the Can-Can music if you sing it (roughly!) In writing this, the composer Saint-Saëns was jokingly emphasising the slowness of tortoises!

Pass the contrasts cards: incorporating Fast/Slow

- Use the **galloping horse** card (fast) and the **tortoise** card (slow). Incorporate one other pair of cards too if you wish.

Singing: *The Dingleden Train* (music: p.67)

- Finish by learning a slow song, *The Dingleden Train* with the help of track 4. Substitute the name '*Dingleden*' with the name of your school if possible.

The Dingleden Train

Oh the Dingleden Train goes chugging along,
Chugging along,
Chugging along.
Oh the Dingleden Train goes chugging along,
'Till the top meets the tip.

- Now stand up (try to get into the habit of giving the instruction 'stand up', 'sit down' with the

musical signal) and find a space. You are going to be the leader for the first time you sing this song. Walk round the room singing the song unaccompanied. Every few seconds touch a child lightly on the head. That child must join in behind you, holding your waist, (or hips if they can't reach!) and join in singing. The 'train' will get longer and longer, and the volume of the singing will gradually increase as each child joins in. When the last child has joined the train, you (the leader) must cut across (rather than endlessly going round and round and never catching up!), to join onto the last person in the line, then all hold hands in a circle.

- Now try the whole song once more, this time choosing one of the children as the leader. The accompaniment for this song is not on the CD because the song is of indeterminate length. So sing it unaccompanied but be careful not to speed up.

The Dingleden Train

Lesson 9

Objective:

- To extend the contrasts work, focusing on absorbing the contrasts: High/Low, Smooth/Jumpy

Signals

- Learn a new signal – **turn around once**. To play this signal, scrape your nails round the skin of a drum.

Listening: *Carnival of the Animals* – focusing on High/Low, Smooth/Jumpy

- Sit down and listen to 'The Elephant'. Notice the very deep sound of the double bass. Point out that this is another member of the string family, the 'daddy'. It normally stands taller than the person who plays it. Generally, the bigger the instrument the lower the sound it produces. The music for 'The Elephant' is not conducive to moving around the room. It is in 3-time. To convey this to the children, try clapping '1, 2, 3' repeatedly, when you can hear the metre. You will always be clapping and saying '1' on the strongest beat. To emphasise this strong beat, try tapping knees on beat number 1 and doing nothing on beats 2 and 3.

- Now listen to 'The Aviary'. Can the children hear the flutes? Are these from the string family or the wind family? Point out the contrast between this very high music and the elephant's very low music.

- Next listen to 'The Kangaroo'. Notice that this is jumpy music, but it doesn't keep to a regular metre. The beats are uneven. Clap in two different ways to demonstrate to the children that the beat can be regular or irregular – first your claps should happen at regular intervals, then irregular. Encourage the children to try that. Listen again to 'The Kangaroo'.

- Listen to 'The Swan'. This is very smooth music, unlike the music heard in 'The Kangaroo'. Do the children recognise the main instrument that is playing the melody? Do they remember that the cello is the 'mummy' of the string family?

Singing: *The Dingleden Train* (p.67)
- Finish with this song if you have time.

Lesson 10

Objectives:
- To consolidate all the contrasts focusing on smooth and slow singing
- To develop rhythmic sense

Signals
- Play a game of this to start the lesson.

A team game using the contrasts cards
- Show the children all the 8 **contrasts cards** and remind them of what each card represents: **soldier** (loud), **creeper** (quiet), **bird** (high), **elephant** (low), **snake** (smooth), **frog** (jumpy), **galloping horse** (fast) and **tortoise** (slow). Divide the class into teams. Each team should form a little circle. Give each team 1 set of the 8 cards. A useful tip is to back the pictures with different colour card for each team.

- Play the children a short extract from *Carnival of the Animals*, such as 'The Aviary'. The children should recognise that this music is High. One child from each team then holds up the picture that they think represents High. Those children holding the **bird** card score a point for their team. If any of the teams choose the **galloping horse** card or the **creeper** card, they also deserve a point, because the music is Fast and Quiet as well as being High. Have a bit of discussion about that point.

- Continue like this, playing any of the extracts that have been heard so far. Get a different child each time to hold up the picture that their team thinks is representative of the music you have just played. See which team gains most points.

Choosing the **elephant** card for Low

Equal claps around the circle
- A new game for rhythm and anticipation.
- Sit in a circle. Going round the circle, each child claps 4 equal beats while saying '1, 2, 3, 4' out loud. There are various pitfalls to try to avoid here: coming in too soon; leaving a gap between 1 set of 4 beats; speeding up during clapping and slowing down during clapping. The children must be alert, anticipating their turn, with their hands ready to clap. Demonstrate by clapping the correct and incorrect way of maintaining these equal beats.

Singing: *The Dingleden Train* (p.67)
- Finish with this song if you have time.

Lesson 11

Objective:
- To develop a sense of rhythm, concentration, co-ordination, anticipation and a feeling of structure, style and mood through music and movement

Signals

- Learn a new signal – **touch your heads**. For this signal play the very top note of the xylophone just once.

A contrasts activity using instruments and action

- See Lesson 7 and try the same activity with **frogs** and **snakes** instead of **soldiers** and **creepers**. Use the same instruments as used in Lesson 7. When you point to the tambourine/tambour/drum group, they should scrape their nails smoothly (legato) around their instruments, and the snakes must glide smoothly round with the music. When you point to the group with the wooden instruments, the other group must instantly stop playing and the snakes return to base. The wooden instruments should play staccato (short notes), with your help to keep them in time, while the frogs 'jump' around.

Listening: *Carnival of the Animals* – 'Fossils'

- Using the music of 'Fossils', you and the class are going to do some dancing. For now, just learn the 'chorus', which is the recurring melody in this piece. (There will be a chance to revisit *Carnival of the Animals* in Year 2, when the children will learn a full choreography to this piece.)
- The piece starts with the 'chorus'. It comes up four times in total, the last one being a shorter version. In between choruses, the children should 'freeze' and listen, trying to anticipate the next chorus.
- Try the dance a few times through. The children will enjoy developing their memory skills!
- At the end of the dance talk about the music that the children listened to while 'frozen'. Did they spot any contrasting elements?

Choreography of the chorus

- Stand straight with feet slightly apart, wrists at chest level, hands dangling. Keeping with the beat:
  1. shake fingers (8 beats)
  2. kick out the right foot, put it down, then kick out the left foot and put it down, then repeat (8 beats)
  3. move the head from side to side in a 'tick-tock' motion (8 beats)
  4. bend and straighten the knees four times (8 beats)
- For the last chorus, which is shorter, just do the shakes and two of the kicks then do a grand bow to finish.

Singing: *Jump!* (p.66)

- If time, finish with this song (track 2).

Lesson 12

Objective:
- Consolidation

Additional resource: A blindfold

A Christmas signals game

- For this seasonal alternative, the *type* of percussion instrument you play represents each signal. When you play:
  Shaker: The children should sway with arms stretched up above their heads to show the tall fir trees that Father Christmas' sleigh brushes as he flies through the sky.
  Finger cymbals: The children should stand in the shape of a star in the night sky.
  Xylophone (running beater from top to bottom): The children should pretend they are skiing down the snowy slopes like Father Christmas.
  Drum (3 loud taps): The children should mime putting their heavy sacks on their backs like Father Christmas.
  Bells: The children should curl up asleep on the floor.

Listening: *Carnival of the Animals*

- First repeat the dance to the music of 'Fossils'.
- Now play 'The Grand Finale'. Combine any of the following actions, keeping in time to the beat throughout:
  marching round the room
  tapping knees
  'conducting' the music
  clapping in time

- Change from one action to the next whenever you want. If you feel a new musical sentence beginning, this is a good time for a change. You might want to lead the children by introducing each new action yourself for them to copy, or you might want to demonstrate the actions once at the beginning and then let the children move freely.

Equal claps around the circle

- Have a game of this.

Singing: *It's Me!* (p.67)

- If time, finish with this song.

Chapter 2
Year 1, Term 2

Theme: Action!

Concept: Note values (notes of short, medium and longer length)

Medium-term objective:
- To continue to develop listening, rhythmic and concentration skills with the emphasis on three note values – crotchets, minims and quavers

Music to listen to: *The Sorcerer's Apprentice* by Paul Dukas

Songs: *Spiller Teddy's Wellies; The Hokey Cokey; The Teeth Pop Up!; I'm Fred Wheelie Bin* and your own choice of songs, if required

Resources: CD; a wide range of percussion instruments; 8 of each type of note value card (except semibreves) and your own choice of songs, if required; CD of *The Sorcerer's Apprentice* and *Carnival of the Animals*

Lesson 13

Objective:
- To start to learn, understand, recognise, step and clap the three note values – crotchets, minims and quavers

Don't worry about the apparent length of this lesson. It is a lot of information that condenses into a normal length lesson!

Signals
- Start with this game as a warm up.

Walking with regular even steps at three different speeds
- Remind the children of the contrast Fast/Slow (Lesson 8). From now on we're going to have Fast, *Medium* and Slow, and instead of animals, people are going to be used to represent the different speeds. The different speeds are indicated on the CD, tracks 5 to 7.

Mummies' notes
- Choose a natural walking pace, taking care to stick to it and walk round the room. 'Here is Medium Mummy walking to work.' Encourage the children to walk with you at exactly the same speed. Walk in time with track 5 on the CD. Here the tambourine plays the **mummies' notes**.

- Now try it *without* the CD. While the children continue walking at that speed, you tap those same even mummies' notes on a pair of claves. Whenever a child is showing particularly good listening by starting, stopping or stepping in time accurately, ask them to demonstrate.

Great-Grandads' notes
- Now show the children how Great-Grandads walk much more slowly. Each step you take must look and feel as natural as possible (legato rather than staccato!), and must be *exactly twice as slow* as a mummies' step. Using track 6, encourage the children to join in with you. They will find it difficult to walk so slowly at first. Listen for the wood block which is playing **great-grandad's notes** and try to walk in time with this.

- As before, try it without the CD. The children walk round at this same slow speed while you play the claves to match. If anyone is stepping perfectly in time to your beat, ask him or her to demonstrate. The other children should watch this child's feet, listen to your beat and join in clapping at exactly the same speed.

Alternate stepping and clapping – mummies' notes
- Go back to playing mummies' notes (exactly twice as fast as great-grandads' notes, remember) for the children to step around the room to. When they hear you swap to another percussion instrument they must stand still and clap at the same speed. (Have a tambourine handy so you can simply

tap one of the claves lightly on the tambourine, to avoid a break in the beats when you change instruments.)

Children's notes

- Now demonstrate **children's notes**. Jog, rather than run, because the less ground you cover, the more easily you will be able to stop at precisely the right moment. Point this out to the children. It is essential that your jogging speed is exactly twice as fast as the mummies' notes. Encourage the children to join in. A series of children's notes are played by a shaker on track 7. As before, walk around the room to the CD and then continue without it. Next try it with you playing the note value on alternate instruments. When they hear you change to the tambourine they should stand still and clap at the same speed.

Mixing these three speeds

- Now mix up the three speeds in any order. Give the children an example first. Always do claves followed by the tambourine *but at the same speed*, before moving to a different speed. Remember, if you change from great-grandads' notes to children's notes you will be tapping 4 times as fast, or if you change from children's notes to great-grandads' notes, 4 times as slow. Track 8 gives one example of what you might play – try it out beforehand. Each note value is played in the following order:

  16 mummies' notes
  8 great-grandads' notes
  16 mummies' notes
  32 children's notes
  16 mummies' notes

- Try it without counting. Because the example has 16 beats duration for each note value, it is easy to anticipate when to change. You will instinctively change from claves to tambourine and from one note value to another, when you have tried it out a couple of times.

Learning the proper names for these notes

- Show the children the picture of a mummies' note (from the back of the book). The proper music name for this is CROTCHET.

a crotchet

- Next show a great-grandads' note. The proper music name for this is MINIM.

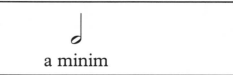

a minim

- Then show a card with two children's notes. The proper music name for these is QUAVERS. Children's notes or quavers always come in pairs, 'holding hands' so there are two quavers on the card. (Much later quavers come singly, but it is best not to confuse the issue here.)

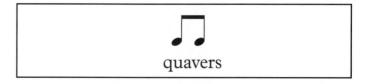

quavers

- Separate the two syllables of the word 'quaver' as you clap and say them repeatedly at the right speed. Try this with the other two note values too. Get the children to join in. This helps to learn the names, while reinforcing the three speeds at the same time.

It is important for you to realise here that these three note values are actually durations, rather than speeds. If we were being accurate we would only ever play the notes on an instrument that could sustain each note until the next one – such as cymbals, a glockenspiel, piano, keyboard or chime bar. If played on a drum or using claves, the sound stops abruptly and doesn't ring on. It is most noticeable with minims. Playing a series of minims, the sound of each minim note should really last until the next one is played. However, at this stage it is more sensible for the children to simply recognise and understand the three comparative speeds, which is why I'm not insisting on the correct duration of note each time. We'll come back to it later in the course.

Pass the notes round the circle

- The children sit in a circle. Play any track used last term from *Carnival of the Animals*, while the children pass a **crotchet** card around the circle. When the music stops the child holding this card must walk once round the circle in time to your crotchet beat on the claves, while the others clap in time. Repeat this a few times.
- Now pass the **quaver** card round. When the music stops the child holding the card must jog round the circle while you play quaver beats on the claves (twice as fast) and the others clap in time. Repeat this a few times.
- Now try it with the **minim** card, only this time the child holding the card should take minim steps straight across the circle in time with your minim

beats, and sit down at the other side. (It takes too long to go all the way round the circle!) This is the most difficult one. You might like to give all the children another practice of going round the room stepping out minim beats. Any child stepping particularly well can demonstrate.

- Try this game of **pass the notes round the circle** using all three cards. For this, the children holding the cards when the music stops must listen carefully for which speed you have chosen to tap, to know whose turn it is. You might only play minims for example, then stop and start passing the cards around the circle again. Or you might play a number of quavers followed by a number of crotchets without a break in between, giving two children a go at stepping. Or you could try playing all three to give all three children a go. Repeat this game a few times.

Fossils dance

- Finish with dancing to the 'Fossils' music from *Carnival of the Animals*. See Lesson 11 for a reminder, if required.

Lesson 14

Objective:

- To continue to develop understanding and feeling of the three note values and an awareness of pulse; singing, clapping and moving

Stepping and clapping note values

- Tap claves followed by a tambourine, as in the last lesson, improvising your own combination of the three note values.

Pass the notes round the circle

- Remind the children of the names of the note values before you start.

Singing: *Spiller Teddy's Wellies* (music: p.68)

- Learn this new song with the help of track 9. Notice that the melody 'jogs' along and mainly uses quavers.

Spiller Teddy's Wellies

1. I'm a yellow wobbly jelly and I live in a welly.
   It's Spiller Teddy's welly
   And it's just a little smelly.
   But me and Spiller Teddy,
   We don't care!

   When we walk down the avenue,
   People say 'Haven't you got one funny welly
   'Cause it's full of yellow jelly'.
   But me and Spiller Teddy,
   We don't care!

2. I'm a purple wobbly jelly and I live in a welly.
   It's Spiller Teddy's welly
   And it's just a little smelly.
   But me and Spiller Teddy,
   We don't care!

   When we walk down the avenue,
   People say 'Haven't you got one funny welly
   'Cause it's full of purple jelly'.
   But me and Spiller Teddy,
   We're a pair!

Singing is a very valuable part of children's musical education. The voice is an instrument, and training is just as important when learning to use the voice as it is when learning to play any other instrument. Last term the songs were largely action songs. While singing these songs, the children were enjoying the activity of communal singing, feeling the mood, the style and the beat of the song while co-ordinating actions as they sang. Spiller Teddy's Wellies is the first song in this course where the children should simply sit still and sing. So this is a good moment to establish good singing technique.

Ask the children to sit up straight, cross-legged but without folding their arms. I encourage them to open their mouths wide and try to make a nice sound. You could have half of the class listening to the other half to generate some discussion: Was the singing too loud, too 'shouty' or too whispery? Did the voices 'match' the mood of the song – bright, smooth, sweet, strong, staccato? Were the children pronouncing the words carefully and keeping in time with the accompaniment? Did they know all of their words? Did they start singing at the right moment? It is a good idea to save consideration of breathing technique until Key Stage 2, although I do always talk about the lungs in connection with sitting up straight.

Stepping note values in groups

- Divide the class into three groups and sit them in three corners of the room. Place a different note value on the floor in front of each group. If you tap a series of crotchet beats, the children with that card should stand up and join in stepping crotchets round the room. The moment they hear you change, to another speed they must quietly return to their base and sit down so that the other children can hear which note value you have changed to, and that group steps round accordingly. Give each group two turns randomly, then play your established swap signal to indicate that the groups should move round to the next corner. Each group will now have a new note value to listen out for as you continue the game.

Singing: *Spiller Teddy's Wellies* (p.68)

- If you have time, finish with a quick run through of *Spiller Teddy's Wellies*. Use track 9 again, or track 10 for the accompaniment only.

Lesson 15

Objective:

- To continue to develop understanding and feeling of the three note values

Signals and/or stepping and clapping note values

- For the rest of this term start each lesson with either or both of these activities.

Stepping note values in groups

- Divide the class into three groups and do this activity as before.

Playing note values in groups

- Now give each group a set of instruments, such as tambourines/tambours for the group with the **crotchet** card, claves/wood blocks for the group with the **quaver** card and maracas/shakers for the group with the **minim** card. (I usually find that if the children tap the shaker onto the palm of their other hand, it helps them to produce an accurate beat.) Repeat the activity with the children *playing* the instruments instead of stepping. They should calmly swap places, as before, so each group gets the chance to play at three different speeds. You play a percussion instrument to play the note values and to keep them 'in time'. Don't forget the established swap signal!

Playing note values in groups

Singing: *The Dingleden Train* (p.67)

Lesson 16

Objective:

- To clap or play the three note values while listening to a song

Signals and/or stepping and clapping note values

Singing: *Spiller Teddy's Wellies* (p.68)

- Sing this song using the CD, track 9.
- Now play the song again and all gently clap along with crotchet beats. Clapping through one verse only should be enough to get the idea. See the first line of words below to know when to clap the crotchet beats:

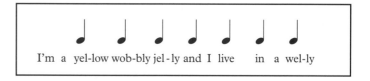

- Now play the song again and accompany with quaver claps (at twice the crotchet speed):

- Next play the track and accompany with crotchet beats again. Then try it a fourth time and clap minim beats:

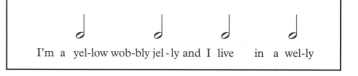

- Extend this activity by holding up one of the three **note value cards**. The children must try to clap at the right speed, then change their speed according to which card you show them next and so on. This time you will need to play through the whole song.
- Now divide the children into three groups, in three corners of the room, and give each group a different **note value card**. Play the CD, track 10. This is the piano accompaniment to *Spiller Teddy's Wellies*, arranged in 11 obvious sections. Accompany it as follows, each group clapping the note value on their card:
  1. quaver group
  2. crotchet group
  3. minim group

4. The three groups move round one place
5. The new **quaver** group
6. The new **crotchet** group
7. The new **minim** group
8. The three groups move round another place
9. The new **quaver** group
10. The new **crotchet** group
11. The new **minim** group

Singing: *The Hokey Cokey* (music: p.69)

- On the CD, track 11 plays the song through five times. The words are the traditional ones that you will know, but some of the actions are different. See below:

The Hokey Cokey

You put your *right arm* in,
You put your *right arm* out.
In, out, in, out,
You shake it all about.
You do the hokey cokey
And you turn around,
And that's what it's all about!

Oh, hokey, cokey, cokey!
Oh, hokey, cokey, cokey!
Oh, hokey, cokey, cokey!
And that's what it's all about!

*2. left arm
 3. right leg
 4. left leg
 5. whole self

Actions
The actions are the traditional ones for the first part of the song. Follow those below for the rest of the piece.

You do the hokey cokey
cross the arms over the chest, one arm at a time to make an 'X' and then uncross them, one arm at a time
Turn around
turn around once
And that's what it's all about
turn the palms of your hands upwards
Oh hokey cokey cokey
raise both arms up high, fingers reaching up to the ceiling. On the second 'cokey' do three small jumps on the spot and at the same time pull arms down in front of you, keeping the forearms vertical, with palms facing towards you to clench each fist. Repeat this for these three lines.
And that's what it's all about
turn the palms of your hands upwards

- The children stand in a space of their own. Spend a bit of time checking that everyone knows which is their right arm, left arm, right leg and left leg. It might be an idea for you to face them and mirror them.

Lesson 17

Objectives:

- To consolidate the three comparative speeds in a rhythmic framework
- To consolidate the note values with the children taking individual responsibility, recognising and clapping note values accurately

Signals and/or stepping and clapping note values

Singing: *Spiller Teddy's Wellies* (p.68)

- Using the CD, track 10, repeat the group activity from the previous lesson, only this time play percussion instruments instead of clapping.

Magic cards

- This is a great game. Give each child a **note value card**, distributing cards of each of the three note values fairly equally amongst the class. Every child sits in a space and looks at his/her card, remembers it, then puts the card face down on the floor. At no point during the game is anyone allowed to show anyone else their card! The aim of the game is for the cards to 'magically' group themselves together according to note values. For example, all children with a **quaver** card should end up together. To achieve this, play a repeated note value on claves. The children must listen and recognise whether or not you are playing the note value of *their* card. If they think you are, they stand up and join in clapping at the same speed. After a few claps group those children together, making sure they keep their cards faced down. Then repeat the whole process with the other two note values. When finished, look at all the cards of each group to see if like cards have 'magically' grouped together. Count how many mistakes there are and see if the class can make it fewer the next time. Play the note values in a different order each time.

25

The **quaver** group

Singing: *The Hokey Cokey* (p.69)
- Use the CD, track 11.

Lesson 18

Objectives:
- To co-ordinate actions and singing
- To develop memory skills
- To reinforce the three note values

Signals and/or stepping and clapping note values

Singing: *The Teeth Pop Up!* (music: p.70)
- Listen to the CD, track 12 to learn the song.

The Teeth Pop Up

The teeth pop up
And the teeth pop down,
And the teeth turn around all day.
The dentist's getting mad
'Cause the teeth are very bad,
And the one on the end keeps running away!

- Now try singing it unaccompanied and clap crotchets at the same time. Can the class think of another action that they can do at the same crotchet speed to accompany the song, instead of clapping? Marching on the spot, for example. Or something more complicated, like four marches, then four head taps?
- Now sing the song unaccompanied again, this time clapping minims throughout. How about trying an alternative minim action, such as bending the knees on the first minim then straightening on the second and continuing like that?
- Divide the class into two groups, one at each end of the room, facing each other. Listen to *The Teeth*

Pop Up! on the CD, track 13. There are six play-throughs. Can the children count them? You and the children will need to think about the actions they want to do, then follow the format below to sing the song.
1. All sing while group one does a pre-set crotchet action throughout.
2. All sing while group two does a pre-set minim action throughout.
3. All march round the room, to swap places.
4. All sing while group two does a pre-set crotchet action throughout.
5. All sing while group one does a pre-set minim action throughout.
6. All sing while both groups do their actions throughout. Group one should do the crotchet action for half the song, then change to the minim action on 'the dentist's getting mad...'. Group two should do their minim action for the first part of the song then switch to their crotchet action for the second. This is tricky! Try it out a few times.

Magic cards
- Finish with a game of this if you have time.

Lesson 19

Objectives:
- To co-ordinate actions while singing
- To develop speed of reaction and co-operation skills

Signals and/or stepping and clapping note values

Singing: *The Teeth Pop Up!* (p.70)
- Arrange the children into two rows (or three rows for a big class), all facing the same way. Try singing this song unaccompanied while doing the following fun actions. Keep repeating the song until every child has 'run away'.

The Teeth Pop Up - Actions

The teeth pop up	*reach both arms up*
the teeth pop down	*crouch down and touch the ground*
turn around all day	*turn around*
getting mad	*fold the arms*
very bad	*wag one index finger as if telling someone off*
running away	*the child at the end of the row runs to join the other end*

A game for the 'false teeth'

- All dance freely to 'Fossils' from *Carnival of the Animals*. When you stop the music this means the dentist is returning and the children should sit down quietly in two rows, like a set of false teeth, before you count to ten. Start and stop the music a number of times.

Equal claps around the circle

- Look back to Lesson 10. This time, each child must clap only 2 beats each going round the circle, whilst saying '1, 2' out loud.

Singing: *The Dingleden Train* (track 4/p.67)
or *Spiller Teddy's Wellies* (track 9/p.68)

Lesson 20

Objective:

■ To develop confidence and projection, as well as rhythmic awareness when singing or playing individually and as a group

Signals and/or stepping and clapping note values

Singing: *I'm Fred Wheelie Bin* (music: p.71)

- With the help of the CD, track 14 learn this new song.
- You are going to follow the same pattern of solo/ group as demonstrated on track 14. This is a good opportunity for solo singing, and is as much about confidence and projection as about singing in tune! Choose five volunteers to stand in a row. Use the CD, track 15. The song is played through (without a vocal line) five times. Each soloist should listen carefully to the introduction and try to come in at exactly the right moment. Before you start, it is a good musical exercise to find different names of one syllable, other than 'Fred', for your five soloists to sing. If their own name fits, then use that. The soloists must then remember to use their chosen name when it is their turn to sing. The remaining children should always join in singing at 'And the man in the van…'. Repeat with another five soloists, and so on.
- With the same CD track, try this: each of the five soloists has a percussion instrument. During the 'solo' section of each verse, these children take turns to play either crotchets or minims in time with the music. Then for the rest of the verse all the children join in clapping at the same speed

as the individual child has chosen. It might be ambitious, but you could try singing at the same time!

I'm Fred Wheelie Bin

(Solo)
I'm Fred Wheelie Bin.
I'm standing in a row.
(Group)
And the man in the van says,
'Quick as you can!
There are *four more wheelie bins to go!'

*2. three
 3. two
 4. one
 5. no

Singing: *The Teeth Pop Up!* (p.70)

- Finish with the fun, action version.

Lesson 21

Objective:

■ To listen attentively for several minutes to music with a story, noticing the atmosphere and mood of the music as well as the dynamic contrast

Signals and/or stepping and clapping note values

Listening: *The Sorcerer's Apprentice* by Paul Dukas

- Sit down and tell the children the story of *The Sorcerer's Apprentice*. If you have access to an actual storybook with this story in, then feel free to use it. Don't forget that visual aid is always a great stimulus to children's imaginations.
- **The story:** There once was a Sorcerer (a magician) and an apprentice, a young boy. The Sorcerer has set his apprentice some jobs to do while he is away, however, the boy is feeling lazy and is reluctant to do these. He would rather do magic, despite warnings that this is dangerous for a beginner. One of the jobs involves filling up the huge crocodile jar with water, which will take many trips to and from the river, so the boy tries to remember which spell he has seen the Sorcerer using to get the broom to fly. If he can manage to do that spell, then the broom could be made to fetch and carry the water from the river. However, things get out of hand when the jar

overflows and the broom won't stop, no matter how hard the boy tries. When he chops it in two, both pieces of broom set off to the river with their buckets, and things get even worse. The music becomes louder and stormier, and more and more frantic and chaotic as the crocodiles escape from the jar. The house contents, and eventually the boy himself, swirl around uncontrollably in the water, before the Sorcerer comes home in the nick of time to save the day. He creates order from chaos and tells off the repentant, frightened boy.

- Now tell the story again with the music playing. The music is approximately 12 minutes long, so let the children listen to it all. The tune is very distinctive and is repeated many times throughout the piece. It represents the stiff movement of the magic broom. Discuss with the children what else might be happening in the music at various points of the piece. Encourage imaginative responses as long as they are in keeping with the feel of the music at that time. For example, for the overflowing water the children might suggest words such as spilling, bubbling and gushing. Does a part of the music portray the image of crocodiles snapping their jaws and the swirling of the Sorcerer's magic books floating away on the water? Is there anything else in the jar – such as frogs?

Singing: *I'm Fred Wheelie Bin* (p.71)
- Sing this to finish the lesson (track 15).

Lesson 22

Objective:
- To recognise and feel the mood, atmosphere, pulse and musical contrasts while listening to music

Signals and/or stepping and clapping note values

Listening: *The Sorcerer's Apprentice*
- Dramatise *The Sorcerer's Apprentice* with improvised creative movement as the focus. With the music playing, all pretend to be the boy or the broom, the water or a crocodile, switching from one to the other whenever you want. The children will enjoy feeling involved in the story. At the end you pretend to be the Sorcerer coming home furious, and putting everything right with one wave of your wand!
- Try to find time to do pictures or craft work, always listening to the music for inspiration.

Some children might want to produce an actual representation of a scene from the story, but others might want to express the feeling of mounting chaos and fear in a more abstract way.

Moving to *The Sorcerer's Apprentice*

Singing
- Choose any song learnt so far that needs the most practice!

Lesson 23

Objective:
- To develop looking, listening and concentration skills

Signals and/or stepping and clapping note values

Magic cards

Follow the conductor
- All the children sit in a space, each with a percussion instrument. You are the conductor. The children must keep looking at you all the time so they know what you want them to do. If you want them to play in unison have a pre-set signal to indicate this, such as drawing a circle in the air. Move your hand up and down in the air like a conductor to show the speed you want them to play. When you want this to stop, put up both hands for silence. If you want only one person to play you should point at that person. If you decide not to indicate a beat, the child can play their instrument as they want. If you point to someone else without showing the silence sign, then both children will play together. Build up the number of signals you use gradually.

Singing
- Sing whichever song needs the most practice!

28

Lesson 24

Objective:

- Revision. (See the Introduction for the importance of revision)

Signals and/or stepping and clapping note values

Magic cards

Singing

- Sing any of the songs from this term or last term and accompany with actions and/or percussion instruments.

Chapter 3
Year 1, Term 3

Theme: Recycling!

Concept: Rhythm building

Medium-term objectives:

- To continue to develop listening, rhythmic and concentration skills
- To be able to recognise and distinguish visually and aurally between six 4/4 rhythms, to understand how they are built up and to be able to clap/play them confidently and accurately
- To begin to compose

Music to listen to: *A Children's Overture* by Roger Quilter

Songs: *Twinkle, Twinkle Little Star*; *I Hear Thunder*; *Frère Jacques*; *Hot Cross Buns*; *Billy Bind*; *Introducing Michael Finnigan to the Recycling Point!*; revisiting *The Hokey Cokey* and your own choice of songs, if required

Resources: CD; all note value cards including 8 semibreves; white/black board; a wide range of percussion instruments; CD of *A Children's Overture*

Lesson 25

Objective:

- To be able to build the first two rhythms, recognise and distinguish visually and aurally between them and clap them confidently and accurately

Extending stepping and clapping note values

- Extend the exercise as follows. Tap crotchets in two different ways – loudly and quietly. Take care to keep the speed exactly the same each time. If you play quietly the children must tiptoe round, if you play loudly they should march. They should clap quietly or loudly when you change from claves to tambourine, as usual.
- Minims can also be played in two different ways. If you play loudly the children should stride heavily, like a giant, if you play quietly they should walk like a great-grandad as before. Stress that the speed does not change just because the taps are louder or quieter.
- One more variation: listen to the rhythm your feet make when you skip; long, short long, short long, short long, etc. When you tap this rhythm the children should skip. They will find it difficult to clap in exactly the same rhythm so they can just clap crotchets if they want.
- So now stepping and clapping incorporates six

possibilities instead of three:

1. tiptoeing
2. marching (both of these are stepping to crotchet beats)
3. giant strides
4. slow walking (both of these are stepping to minim beats)
5. jogging (this is stepping to a quaver beat)
6. skipping (this is stepping to a natural skipping beat)

Rhythm building

- Ask four children to stand in a row in front of the other children. Give each of the four children a **crotchet** card. Each child represents 1 count (or beat). While pointing to each card (so the children watching see you point from left to right, as though spelling out a word) say EGGS AND BA-CON, emphasising the four syllables.

Tell the children that whenever they see four crotchets side by side like this, it is EGGS AND BA-CON. Point again while all the children clap the crotchet rhythm. Pick another four children to hold the cards. Pat knees, tap the floor, tap heads, do anything! for 4 beats while saying EGGS AND BA-CON.

- Now take away the last 2 crotchets, saying you are taking away the BA-CON. Give the third child a minim and leave the fourth child *without* a card. Explain to the children, 'I'm not giving James (fourth child) anything because the minim lasts for 2 crotchet beats so it will last for Harry (third child) and James.' The minim is the HAM. So now it says EGGS AND HAM, stretching out the sound HAM so it lasts for 2 beats.

EGGS AND HAM

EGGS   AND   HAM

- On the board, write either 4 crotchets or 2 crotchets and a minim (as above). Can the children recognise which food words your written notes represent? Now play one of the rhythms (foods) on any instrument without saying the words. Can they tell which it is?

Analysing the rhythm of *Twinkle, Twinkle Little Star* (with recycled words!)

- Divide the class into four groups. Two groups sit down with you to watch, the other two go to the two ends of the room. Set out EGGS AND BA-CON (4 **crotchet** cards) on the floor in front of one group, and EGGS AND HAM (2 **crotchet** cards and a **minim** card) on the floor in front of the other. These two groups take turns to clap their rhythms without a break keeping a steady speed. The children watching should comment on whether the children came in at the right moment and how accurately they clapped. Did the rhythms run on from one group to the next? (A pitfall here is the EGGS AND BACON group coming in before the HAM has had its full 2 beats.) Now

swap over the groups so those who were watching can have a go.

- Next divide the class into two big groups and take turns clapping the two rhythms alternately, having six goes each. This makes the complete rhythm of *Twinkle, Twinkle Little Star*. Following the letters below, reading from left to right, play the tune on the xylophone while the children clap. You might want to try this out beforehand. Do they recognise it?

C	C	G	G	A	A	G
F	F	E	E	D	D	C
G	G	F	F	E	E	D
G	G	F	F	E	E	D
C	C	G	G	A	A	G
F	F	E	E	D	D	C

- Write the rhythm out (*without* the above letters) on the board and point your way through it, as the children sing first the proper words of *Twinkle, Twinkle Little Star* and then the nonsense food words (unaccompanied). Before the next music lesson, if you have a few minutes, ask the children if they can remember which two rhythms they need for *Twinkle, Twinkle Little Star*? Maybe they could try writing out the complete rhythm themselves?

- Play the first four notes (C C G G) again on the xylophone. Can the children think of another nursery rhyme that starts like this? (*Baa, Baa, Black Sheep*.) Sing the answer all together (unaccompanied).

- Do you remember the very first music lesson? The children tapped their first names on a drum round the circle. Repeat that activity, noticing if any of the names match either the EGGS AND BA-CON rhythm (e.g. Alexander) or the EGGS AND HAM rhythm (e.g. Caroline).

Singing: *The Dingleden Train* (p.67)
- Finish with this song if you have time.

Lesson 26

Objective:
- To learn a third rhythm and incorporate it with two others

Extended stepping and clapping note values
- Start with this exercise mixing up the six possible movements as you want.

31

The third food rhythm

SAU - SA - GES AND BA - CON

- Ask four children to stand up in front of the class. Ask another child to hand each of the four children the right cards to make EGGS AND HAM and then to make EGGS AND BA-CON. Clap these two rhythms. Now take away the first 2 crotchets and ask the children what's left. They should say 'BA-CON'. Give the first and second children each a **quaver** card. Tap each note of the quavers (2 taps per card). The rhythm now reads SAU-SA-GES AND BA-CON. All clap and say that.

SAUSAGES AND BACON

- Have four different children stand at the front of the class. Choose someone to hand the right cards to each child to make up SAU-SA-GES AND BA-CON. Are they right? Choose someone else to change it to one of the other two rhythms.
- Clap one of the three rhythms learnt so far. Can the children recognise which one you clapped? Choose one child to give the right cards to each of the four children.

These kinds of activities can be done at any time. They help develop aural and visual understanding and memory of the three rhythms. Devise team games based on the activities.

Matching the children's names to the three known food rhythms

- Go round the circle, each child tapping the drum as they say their full name. Does anyone have a name that sounds like SAU-SA-GES AND BA-CON? For example, A-lex-an-dra Thom-son or O-li-ver Mac-do-nald. It doesn't matter how the syllables are distributed between the first and last names, it is purely the overall pattern of sound that counts. However, try not to alter the natural flow of a name. For example, Rebecca Moloney has six syllables but we don't say the name with a strong beat on the first syllable, **Re**becca, we say Re**be**cca. So this name does not fit the rhythm of SAU-SA-GES AND BA-CON.

Magic cards

Singing: *The Hokey Cokey* (p.69)

- Try using the CD, track 16 this time, which is the piano accompaniment only.

Lesson 27

Objective:

- To deepen understanding of the three known rhythms

Extended stepping and clapping note values

- Revise the activity from the last lesson.

Revising the three known food rhythms

- Using ideas from the beginning of Lesson 26 (where four children stand in a row at the front representing the 4 counts/beats), we are going to deepen the children's understanding of the three rhythms.
- Divide the class into four groups and give each group similar percussion instruments. You might give claves to one group, tambourines to the next group, shakers to the third group and tambours to the last group. Set out the **note value cards** on the floor in front of each group in the following way:

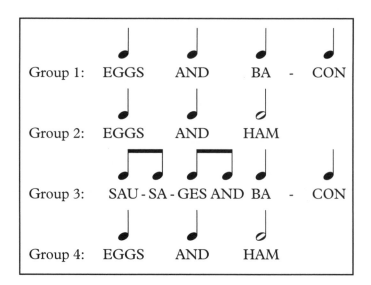

Analysing the rhythm *I Hear Thunder/Frère Jacques* **(with recycled words!)** (music: p.72)

- Each group, one to four, should play their rhythm twice without a break, making sure they follow straight on from the previous group. Group three must take care not to interrupt the second beat of Group two's minim (HAM), by coming in too soon. You play exactly what the children are playing on the xylophone, playing a different note for each group so you might play EGGS AND BA-CON twice on the note A, then EGGS AND HAM twice on the note C and so on. Then change to tapping a drum very lightly for the children to tiptoe round one place so they move onto a different group. Repeat the whole routine four times in all, giving each group the chance to play all four types of instrument.
- Can anybody recognise, just from the rhythm, that this is *I Hear Thunder* (or they may say *Frère Jacques*, which has the same tune). Sing both these songs unaccompanied. Do actions for the words of *I Hear Thunder*.
- Write out the rhythm in full on the board and point your way through it as everybody sings first, the words to *I Hear Thunder*, then the nonsense food words.

```
I Hear Thunder

I hear thunder,
I hear thunder.
Hush, don't you?
Hush, don't you?
Pitter patter rain drops,
Pitter patter raindrops.
I'm wet through,
So are you!
```

```
Frère Jacques

Frère Jacques,
Frère Jacques,
Dormez vous?
Dormez vous?
Sonnez les matines,
Sonnez les matines.
Ding, dang, dong,
Ding, dang, dong.
```

Singing: *The Dingleden Train* (p.67) **and/or** *The Hokey Cokey* (track 16/p.69)

Lesson 28

Objectives:

- To improvise a whole-class percussion piece
- To develop the skill of listening sensitively in order to contribute an individual sound to a set of sounds
- To memorise rhythmic sequences

A variation on extended stepping and clapping note values

- First practise making a circle with the minimum of fuss. I often say to the children 'The slower you go, the quicker you go!' (my version of 'More haste, less speed!') If they simply reach out their two hands gently and take small steps while looking to join up with someone else, the circle will make itself. Once the circle is made they should sit down.
- Now do **extended stepping and clapping**. This time when you stop tapping, the children must immediately form a 'fuss-free' circle. Try this a few times.

Singing: revising the rhythm for *I Hear Thunder* (p.72)

- First sing the song then ask the children to tell you what to write on the board to create the rhythm of this song.

A whole-class piece – *The Thunderstorm*

- Sit or kneel down in a circle. You are going to make a thunderstorm! First talk about a thunderstorm – the gentle rain becoming heavier, the thunder and lightning, then the passing of the storm. This exercise needs careful listening to judge the CRESCENDO (getting louder) and the DIMINUENDO (getting softer).
- All tap very gently with curved fingertips on the floor. By tapping harder make the taps gradually louder, then point to each child indicating to them when they can tap with their whole hands. Allowing one child to join in at a time with the hard tapping creates a gradual increase in volume. This is the thunder. Now the storm is passing over, so again, point to individual children who should change from tapping with their whole hand to using their fingertips. This means the children must be watching you all the time. You are the conductor. When everyone is tapping with their fingers, you should all tap more and more softly listening carefully to judge the diminuendo. And finally tap with just one finger for the last few drops more and more quietly until there is silence. Take a few seconds to feel this silence at the

end. Just as sounds have quality, so does silence. Repeat the exercise, encouraging the children to listen carefully to the gradation of the tone and to the mood of the piece.

Translating *The Thunderstorm* on to percussion instruments

- We are going to try IMPROVISING a percussion piece called *The Thunderstorm*, transfering what you did with the finger and hand sounds, to instruments. Discuss which instruments would be appropriate to fit the sounds of a storm or the way a storm makes you feel and give each child one instrument. Apart from wooden sounds, any instrument will work. Cymbals and drums work well for the thunder while sharp 'raps' on one cymbal, using a beater, creates a good lightning effect. Remind the children with cymbals to hold the cymbal away from their bodies when playing it. This activity leaves lots of room for interpretation, so go for it! Try to control the gradation of the crescendo and the diminuendo. Encourage the children to be aware of their personal contribution to the effect of the whole piece. They will need to be looking and listening all the time. Try to create a definite beginning, middle and end. The beginning would be the first rain drops drizzling then becoming heavier, the middle would be the thunder and lightening raging, and the end would be the storm passing over and dying away. Record the piece, when you have had a practice.

- Before you discuss your recording, see how well the children were listening *while* they were playing. Did anyone notice an imbalance of sound? For example, someone banging away on a tambourine not realising that his or her sound was 'sticking out', or someone whose instrument was never heard. Another valid comment might be that there was an imbalance in the structure. Maybe the beginning or the end was too long/short for the middle. Now play back the recording and make further observations.

- Listen again. Can you think of ways to improve your piece?

Lesson 29

Objective:

■ To learn a fourth rhythm and incorporate it with the other three

Another variation on stepping and clapping note values

- This time when you stop playing for the stepping and clapping the children should listen to how many rings you do on the finger chimes – 2 means get into pairs, 3, get into threes etc. The children should only sit down when they have the right number of people in their group. Try to choose a number of chimes that is compatible with your class size!

A new food rhythm: SAUSAGES AND HAM

SAU - SA - GES AND HAM

- Have four children standing in front of the others. Give each of the first two children a **quaver** card, and the third one a **minim** card. The fourth child won't need anything because of the 2 beat duration of the minim. See if the children can work out what this rhythm says. (It is SAU-SA-GES AND HAM).

Responding to food rhythms in groups

- Now divide the class into four groups and hand each group percussion instruments and a set of cards for one of the four food rhythms (don't tell them what it is, they must work it out). Choose any percussion instrument yourself and repeatedly play one of the rhythms. As soon as the children recognise what you are playing they should join in chanting the rhythm, but *only* the group who has the right cards for that rhythm should *play* it with you. After a few play-throughs, have a very short pause then play a different rhythm. When you have played all four rhythms at random, play gentle crotchet taps on the drum for the children to move round to the next set of cards. Allow them some time to work out what their new rhythm is before starting again. Continue like this.

Does anyone's name match SAUSAGES AND HAM?

- Sitting in a circle, pass a drum around the circle, with each child tapping on the drum as they say their full name. Does anybody's name match the rhythm of SAU-SA-GES AND HAM? For example, Ga-bri-el-la Brown.

Singing: *The Hokey Cokey* (with a difference!) (p.69)
- Use the CD, track 16 which is the accompaniment. Instead of singing the words, 'and you turn around' sing an alternative for each of the five sing-throughs. Use the words and actions suggested below or invent your own:
  1. and you clap 3 times
  2. and you tap your heads
  3. and you pat your knees
  4. and you touch your toes
  5. and you swing your hips
  This is good for developing memory skills!

Lesson 30

Objectives:
- To listen for familiar tunes hidden in unfamiliar music and to apply this idea to a class composition

Combining the two variations of extended stepping and clapping
- The children should listen for the chimes when the stepping and clapping stops, as in the previous lesson. This time, if you play only one chime, the children must form a 'fuss-free' circle. 2 taps means getting into pairs, 3 into groups of three, etc.

Listening: *A Children's Overture* by Roger Quilter
- This piece is approximately 11 minutes long, but it is so full of interest that the children should be able to listen to it all in one go, especially if they have something to do! The piece comprises various nursery rhymes cleverly woven together and sometimes almost hidden in the music. It might be an idea for you to listen to the music on your own first, to hear how each tune blends into the next one.
- At the very beginning all stand in a space. When you hear a few notes from *Baa, Baa, Black Sheep*, salute, stand very still and wait for…
  Girls and Boys Come Out To Play. As soon as it starts, the children should skip round the room, listening out for the tambourine. But the moment it changes to
  Bells Ringing upon Paul's Steeple they should all sit down. (It's easy to recognise this bit

because it sounds like church bells ringing).
Dame Get Up and Bake Your Pies starts, and the children should calmly and slowly form a class circle, holding hands and standing still. Next it's
I Saw Three Ships which is played on the viola (like a violin, but with a deeper tone). During this bit the children should walk slowly round in their circle, waiting for the music to change into a lively
Sing A Song Of Sixpence. The children should all trot round for this section, but you need lots of energy because it's fast! Now sit down for the lovely, sombre
There Was A Lady Loved A Swine, and rock gently from side to side until
Over the Hills and Far Away begins on the flute. This is also very light and fast. Listen for the tambourines as you hold hands with a partner and dance round.
The Crow and the Frog follows, played on the oboe at first. Sit down until
A Frog He Would A-Wooing Go, which reminds me of a big fat frog jumping about! Can the children jump around the room like this? They should pause in between each jump, and listen for the tambourine again. Then it's
Baa, Baa, Black Sheep. Lie down for this section and enjoy the smooth calm tune.
Here We Go Round the Mulberry Bush follows on the piccolo. Stand up and tiptoe round to the very rhythmic beat, but get ready to stop and salute for
Oranges and Lemons. This gets gradually faster and leads into
Boys and Girls Come Out To Play. Skip round until it slows down into the final
Oranges and Lemons (with bits of other tunes!). Stand still and pretend to be a conductor conducting the grand ending!
- Sit down and talk briefly about the music. Roger Quilter started to write this in 1911, then left it a few years and came back to it in 1919. How many nursery rhymes did the children recognise? Which bit did they like best?

An improvisation/composition based on *Twinkle, Twinkle Little Star*
- Let's define the two words IMPROVISATION and COMPOSITION. An IMPROVISATION is invented spontaneously, so unless it is short enough to memorise, it will be difficult to reproduce exactly. Any two performances of a COMPOSITION will always turn out the same, allowing for interpretation (i.e. the tempo and 'colour' of the music might differ). In both you are creating something new.
- The children should form a circle. You join the

circle with a xylophone. Show the children how you are going to play the *opening* notes of *Twinkle, Twinkle Little Star*.

C	C	G	G	A	A	G
F	F	E	E	D	D	C

- Now give every child a percussion instrument, using a wide selection of instruments. You go into the middle of the circle ready to play the xylophone. Start clapping at a steady crotchet speed and all the children must start playing their instruments at that same speed. Choose a child to walk round the outside of the circle during this. As they walk they must watch you carefully. When you stop clapping (and you can stop whenever you want), they should stop walking. Whoever they are standing behind in the circle should play their instrument all on their own. They should play the rhythm to the opening of *Twinkle, Twinkle Little Star*, up to the words, ' how I wonder what you are'. (So they will actually be playing EGGS AND BACON, EGGS AND HAM *twice*.) **At the same time** *you* play those opening notes of *Twinkle, Twinkle Little Star* on the xylophone, so they can hear the tune too. As soon as you've played this, go back to clapping. The children should also resume their crotchet beat on their instruments, except for the child who just played the solo. That child should be the next one to walk round the circle, watching for when you stop clapping again. And so it goes on. Make the length of time you spend clapping vary each time for greater musical interest.
- When you've had a bit of practice, try recording what emerges. Listen to the tape and comment on the sound of your piece. Did everyone play in time? Did the speed stay the same throughout? Which instrument sounded best with the xylophone? Were there any gaps?

Lesson 31

Objectives:

- To learn a fifth food rhythm and incorporate it with the other four
- To listen for specific hidden sounds and to focus on instrumentation

The fifth food rhythm

- Have four children standing in front of the others. Give these children the right cards for SAU-SA-

GES AND BA-CON. Take away the 2 crotchets, saying you are taking away the BA-CON. Give these two children each a **quaver** card so all the children have quavers. The rhythm now says SAU-SA-GES AND BREAD AND BU-TTER. All clap and say this.

SAU - SA - GES AND BREAD AND BUT-TER

Analysing the rhythm of *Hot Cross Buns* (music: p.73)

- Divide the children into eight groups. Put **note cards** on the floor in front of each group as follows:
  1) EGGS AND HAM
  2) EGGS AND HAM
  3) SAUSAGES AND BREAD AND BUTTER
  4) EGGS AND HAM
  5) SAUSAGES AND BACON
  6) SAUSAGES AND HAM
  7) SAUSAGES AND BREAD AND BUTTER
  8) EGGS AND HAM

  Ask the children to take turns clapping their rhythm just once through, following straight on to the next group without a break. Does anyone recognise what song this rhythm makes? The answer is *Hot Cross Buns*.
- Write the rhythm on the board *without the words* and tap it through as the children sing *Hot Cross Buns*, first to the proper words, then to the nonsense food words.

Listening: *A Children's Overture*

- Sit still and listen to this piece again. If you have any pictures of the featured instruments listed below, show these as you listen.
- The viola, which plays *I Saw Three Ships*, looks like a large violin, but sounds slightly deeper. The flute plays *Over the Hills and Far Away*. The oboe plays *The Crow and the Frog*. The piccolo plays *Here We Go Round the Mulberry Bush*.

A great new game – find Michael Finnigan!

- Select one person to be 'The Listener'. Ask them to go to the side of the room and hide their eyes, while you choose one of the other children to be Michael Finnigan. All the children sit down in their own space except the listener. When you say '1, 2, 3, go!', all the children start saying their own name loudly over and over again, except one who says 'Michael Finnigan'. The listener must try to 'pull' this sound from all the rest by focusing their listening. How quickly can they find Michael

Finnigan? You will notice that as the children mature and develop their listening skills, they are able to hone in on the sound by 'scan' listening (similar to the way that adults 'skim' read), without having to go right up to each child and listen to them in turn.

Lesson 32

Objective:
■ To consolidate the five known food rhythms

Extended stepping and clapping
• Play the latest variation, but this time when you hit the chime bar once the children should sit down to make a class 'T' shape instead of making a circle.

Consolidating the five known food rhythms
• **Either** play a game of **responding to food rhythms in groups** from Lesson 29. Use all five known rhythms. As the children learn more rhythms you might find it simpler to let the children join in clapping, rather than playing an instrument.

Clapping the rhythm, EGGS AND BREAD AND BUTTER

• **Or** play a team game as follows: Write up all five known rhythms on the board. Point to one of them. Award points to the team(s) who works out correctly (notice I haven't said 'guess' correctly!) which food words match the rhythm to which you are pointing. Award bonus points if anyone can say someone's name that matches.
• An extension to this is to number each rhythm on the board and clap one of them. The answer will therefore be a *number*. The children will find this quite difficult, because it is tempting to simply call out the right food words when they hear you

clap, without matching the sound to the visual representation on the board.
• The skill in both these consolidation games is recognising the sound *and* sight of the food rhythm and making the connection between the two.

Singing: *The Hokey Cokey* (p.69)
• Sing this with the five alternative actions to the line 'and you turn around' from Lesson 29.
• Now ask the children to help you choose a few more actions. Encourage them to use their imaginations. They might think of things like 'be a croc'. For this one make 'crocodile jaws' with arms outstretched in front, one on top of the other, and clap your hands. They might think of 'play guitar' for which the action is self- explanatory. Remember that whatever action they suggest must be said in three syllables to fit to the music.

Lesson 33

Objective:
■ To develop aural discrimination skills

Find Michael Finnigan!
• Start with a few games of this for a change.

Extended magic cards
• Hand all the children either a **crotchet** or a **minim** card. Look back to Lesson 17 (p.25) to check the rules. Tell them you are going to be playing crotchets on a drum and therefore those children with **crotchet** cards must clap at *exactly the same speed as you*. Those with **minim** cards must clap *exactly twice as slowly*. Demonstrate this beforehand. This time when you say 'Go!', all the children are going to clap *at the same time*.
• The children should be looking around as they clap to see who is clapping the same as them. If they see someone else clapping at the same speed, they should go and join them. They should then stand up together and continue to clap. Other children clapping at the same speed will see the group forming and come to join it Gradually two groups should form. (Remind the children to take their cards with them when they move, but they must not show or tell anyone what's on their card). When finished, ask the children to hold up their cards. The 'magic' has worked if *like* cards are *together*.

A new game – if it's your name, run!

- The children sit in a space of their own. You tap one of their names on any instrument. In this initial version of the game, make it easy by saying the name at the same time. In a later version of the game they must recognise their name from the tapping only.

- Then, on another instrument, play either 1, 2 or 3 taps. 1 tap represents **door**, 2 represents **white board**, 3 represents **radio**. (i.e. the number of taps corresponds to the number of syllables). The child whose name you have tapped must simply jump up, run and touch the right place.

Singing: *The Hokey Cokey* (p.69)

- Sing with the CD, track 16. This time, during the section of music which introduces each new sing-through, call out a child's name, and they must call out an action such as 'play gui- tar', 'touch your toes' or 'click, click, click'. (The child's name followed by their calling out of the chosen action should fit exactly into the bit of intro music for the next sing-through, but you have to be ready!) The children (and you!) must remember what they've said and incorporate these words with the relevant action in the next sing-through. So you might sing, 'You do the hokey cokey and you play guitar.'

Lesson 34

Objective:

- To develop aural discrimination skills by extending known games

Signals and/or extended stepping and clapping

- Do any variation of this.

Extended magic cards

- This time use only **crotchet** cards and **quaver** cards. You tap crotchets.

If it's your name, run!

- The extension here is that you *don't* say the child's name as you tap it, so it is much more difficult to recognise.

- You might like to play this as a team game. Divide the class into four teams and give each team the chance to say whose name you played. You can choose any name to play – it is of no significance which team that child is in. (The running to the right place doesn't gain any points for the team but is good listening practice and good fun!)

There might be more than one child whose names sound the same. It is useful to have a class list in front of you and to have worked out which names have the same rhythm beforehand. Any of these children may run.

Recycle *Hot Cross Buns* by composing your own words (music: p.73)

- Below, I have substituted the words of *Hot Cross Buns* with those of *Billy Bind*.

  Billy Bind, Billy Bind.
  Nobody could be as nice as Billy Bind.
  Always really friendly,
  Always really kind.
  Nobody could be as nice as Billy Bind.

- Divide the class into four or five groups. Each group must choose an alternative name to *Billy Bind*. The chosen name must have three syllables e.g. Molly Strong or Jamie Brown etc. You can either help the children to create a rhyme (here it is 'bind' and 'kind'), or dispense with the rhyme at this stage.

- The groups should take turns singing their composition while the other groups listen critically. Talk about the composition and the performance afterwards. Who sang their words most clearly? Who chose a really interesting name? Who sang with a good sense of rhythm?

Find Michael Finnigan!

- Finish with this game if you have time.

Lesson 35

Objective:

- To develop aural discrimination skills, with a focus on rhythm

Extended stepping and clapping

- This time when you hit the chime bar once, the children should sit in the shape of a whole-class 'C'.

Extended magic cards 2

- The extension this time is that you have all three note values in play (minims, crotchets and quavers). You still play crotchets in order to keep the whole thing in time. Explain to the children that if they have a **crotchet** card they are lucky because they simply clap at the same speed as you. The children with **quaver** cards must clap twice as fast as your beat and the children with **minim** cards twice as slowly. This is very tricky and might not work. Never mind! Keep trying!

Singing: *Introducing Michael Finnigan to the Recycling Point* (music: p.74)

- Learn this song with or without the help of track 17 on the CD.
- Now sing it with track 18, which is the accompaniment only. Divide the class into three groups. For each of the three play-throughs on this track, two groups sing and the third group claps or plays percussion to the rhythm of EGGS AND HAM throughout. Swap round so a different group gets to sing/clap/play each time.

Introducing Michael Finnigan to the Recycling Point

There was an old man called Michael Finnigan.
He just loved his wheelie bin-igan.
Always chucking *bottles in again.
Silly old Michael Finnigan, begin again.
Take your *bottles* to the recycling point!

*2. *paper*
 3. *plastic*

---

backwards.
- Have a thorough revision of the six known rhythms, using different sets of four children at the front to hold the cards demonstrating the rhythm.

Responding to food rhythms in groups

- Look back to Lesson 29 and try this with six groups, using the six known food rhythms.

Singing: *Introducing Michael Finnigan to the Recycling Point!* (p.74)

- Sing with the CD track 18. Practise performing this in three groups as in the last lesson.

Lesson 36

Objective:

- To learn a sixth food rhythm and integrate it with the other five

---

If it's your name, run!

- Start with this game for a change. Try it with teams as in Lesson 34. A new place to run to is **radiator** (4 taps).

The sixth food rhythm

EGGS   AND   BREAD AND BUT-TER

- Learn in the same way as usual with four children standing in front of the class holding the cards representing the 4 beats. Point out that this rhythm looks like SAUSAGES AND BACON

Chapter 4
Year 2, Term 1

Theme: Stories

Concept: Pitch (lower and higher notes)

Medium-term objectives:
■ To continue to develop listening, rhythmic and concentration skills
■ To consolidate rhythm building and note values
■ To learn a new note value – the semibreve
■ To understand the new concept of pitch

Music to listen to: *The Nutcracker Suite* by Tchaikovsky

Songs: *What's My Name?* (from *Rumpelstiltskin*); *Bazookas!* (from *Jack and the Beanstalk*); *The Giant's Garden* (from *The Selfish Giant*) and your own choice of songs, if required

Resources: CD; all note value cards; contrasts cards; white/black board; a full range of percussion instruments including Indian bells or finger chimes; CD of *The Nutcracker Suite*; song sheets (optional)

Lesson 1

Objectives:
■ To memorise a simple rhythmic sequence
■ To understand the beginnings of pitch work

Stepping a sequence
• A simple activity to start with. Tap 4 minims followed by 8 crotchets, repeatedly on an instrument of your choice, the children should step around the room *in time* to your beat.

Beginning PITCH
• Using a xylophone you are going to introduce the concept of PITCH (lower and higher notes). The children should sit so they can all clearly see your xylophone. Demonstrate how the notes with the big bars make the low sounds and as the bars get smaller, the sounds get higher. Play all the notes from a lower C to a higher C (choosing Cs within vocal range). All sing the numbers 1 to 8 slowly as you play each note. Then sing down from 8 to 1.

Singing and growing
• Ask the children to kneel, curled over, in a space of their own. They should use the following actions to 'grow' while singing each number from 1 to 8 four times, as you play each of the notes

from low C to high C. Play each note four times.
• C = curled up (1)
  D = kneel with bottom on heels (2)
  E = kneel up (3)
  F = kneel on one knee and one foot (4)
  G = stand, but bent over (5)
  A = straighten up a bit (6)
  B = hands on shoulders, standing upright (7)
  C = reach up high (8)

The 8 positions

• Now play just the lower C followed by the G, and tell the children these are numbers 1 and 5. Can they do the actions for C and G while singing each number four times, as you play these notes on the xylophone?

Learning SO and DO
• In music we call number 1, 'DO' (pronounced

40

'doe'), and number 5, 'SO'. These two musical notes are the most fundamental notes in any piece of music or song. Lots of pieces of music finish on DO and frequently end with going SO to DO which makes the ending sound very final.

- All do the following hand positions as you sing DO and SO repeatedly. Keep playing them at the same time to check you are singing in tune.

 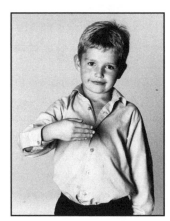

DO   SO

- Sing the tune of *Twinkle, Twinkle Little Star* with the following words. Show the hand signals each time you sing a DO or SO.

DO DO SO SO back to SO
Going down and down to DO
SO SO going down a bit
SO SO going down a bit
DO DO SO SO back to SO
Going down and down to DO

Improvisation/composition based on *Twinkle, Twinkle Little Star*
- Finish the lesson with this (from Year 1, Lesson 30). You might want to revise it first. This time, can one of the children play the xylophone instead of you?

Lesson 2

Objectives:
- To consolidate and develop the memory and pitch work from the last lesson
- To revise the known food rhythms

Stepping a sequence
- Repeat the opening sequence from the previous lesson.

Singing and growing
- Repeat this activity from the last lesson. Can they remember the names and hand signals for number 1 and number 5 (DO and SO)?

Copying three sounds with voice and hand signals
***
- Using the rhythm of EGGS AND HAM, play any combination of the lower C (number 1) and G (number 5). For example, C C G while singing DO DO SO, and doing the correct hand signals with your other hand!
- The children must listen to your voice and watch your hand signal, then copy exactly what you sang with the same hand signals. Do a few examples like this. You might do C G C (DO SO DO), or G G C (SO SO DO), for example.

DO

SO

Revising the six known food rhythms
- Play the team game from Year 1, Lesson 32, where you write the six food rhythms on the board and the children have to match the rhythm to the food name.

Singing: *The Hokey Cokey* (music: p.69)
- Finish by singing this, as in Year 1, Lesson 33 (track 16).

Lesson 3

Objectives:

- To develop memory skills
- To reinforce and develop pitch and rhythm work

Stepping a sequence

- This time extend the sequence you play as follows: 4 minims, 8 crotchets, 16 quavers, 8 crotchets.

Singing and growing

- Try this through a couple of times.

Copying three sounds with voice and hand signals

- Extend this activity as follows. This time when you play the three notes (any combination of C and G) on the xylophone, don't sing the relevant pitch sounds DO and SO, just do the hand signals. Can the children sing the correct notes when they copy?

Singing: *What's My Name?* (music: p.75)

- A new song. With the help of the CD, track 19, learn the first verse and the chorus of *What's My Name?* from the story *Rumpelstiltskin*. The photocopiable song sheet is at the back of the book.

Guess the food rhythms

- Divide the class into three groups. Each group must secretly choose one of the food rhythms. Now play track 20 which is the accompaniment to *What's My Name?* This time, don't sing. Instead, the groups take turns clapping a food rhythm of their choice over and over. Each group accompanies *What's My Name?* once through. At the end, to see who was listening, ask each group if they recognised which food rhythm was being clapped by the other groups. Ask the children to consider whether or not the chosen rhythms a) went well with the music and b) were clapped rhythmically by the group concerned.
- Repeat this activity, each group choosing a different rhythm.

Lesson 4

Objective:

- To learn a seventh food rhythm and incorporate it with the others

Stepping a sequence

- Repeat the extended sequence from the last lesson.

Copying three sounds with voice and hand signals

- Do this activity exactly as in the previous lesson.

Equal claps around the circle

- Look back to Year 1, Lesson 10 and repeat this activity of clapping round the circle, only this time each child claps and says EGGS AND HAM. They must take care not to cut short the previous child's HAM by coming in too soon.

The seventh food rhythm

TOAD   IN THE HOLE

- Have four children standing in front of the others. The first child holds a **crotchet** card, the second child holds a **quaver** card and the third child holds a **minim** card. The fourth child has nothing because the minim lasts for 2 beats. Now clap this through.

Consolidating the seven known food rhythms

- Write up this new rhythm on the board with the others. Play a team game of recognising which rhythm is which.

Singing: *What's My Name?* (p.75)

- With the help of the CD, track 19, revise the first verse of *What's My Name?* and learn the second verse.
- Now divide the class into three groups and give each group different sounding percussion instruments. With the CD, track 20, two groups sing while the third one accompanies by playing the rhythm of TOAD IN THE HOLE. They should only play during the verse. During the chorus, the three groups should move round a place. They can sing the chorus as they move if they like.

Lesson 5

Objective:
- To consolidate food rhythms and extend pitch work

Stepping a sequence
- Repeat the extended sequence from Lesson 3 and then you play the finger chimes to indicate whether the children should get into twos, threes, fours etc. If you play only one chime, the children must look at you to see if you are making a T shape with your hands or a C or an O. This is the whole-class shape they must make.

Copying three sounds with voice and hand signals
- This time see what happens if you only play the notes, so don't sing or give hand signal clues! Can the children *still* recognise which note you are playing, sing the correct SO or DO and make the right hand shape? If not, revert to the previous method of playing and singing!

Equal claps around the circle
- This time each child claps and says TOAD IN THE HOLE.

Clapping back food rhythms
- A new way of consolidating the seven known food rhythms. You clap and say one of the seven known food rhythms. The children must clap and say it straight back to you within a strict rhythmic framework, then you go straight on to the next, and so on.
- Now see if they can still clap and say it back to you if you *don't* say the words as you are clapping.

Singing: *What's My Name?* (p.75)
- With the help of the CD, track 19, learn the last verse of *What's My Name?* Try singing the whole song all the way through with the accompaniment (track 20).

Lesson 6

Objective:
- To consolidate food rhythms

Start with any activity from Year 1
- Choose an activity such as **extended stepping and clapping**, to help develop listening skills.

Responding to food rhythms in groups
- Try this with all seven known rhythms.

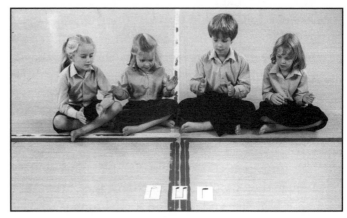

Responding to food rhythms in groups – TOAD IN THE HOLE

Equal claps around the circle
- Take turns to clap and say EGGS AND HAM and TOAD IN THE HOLE alternately.

Singing: *Bazookas!* (music: p.76)
- Start to learn this song with the help of track 21. It was inspired by the story of *Jack and the Beanstalk*. The photocopiable song sheet is at the back of the book.

Lesson 7

Objectives:
- To learn a new note value – the semibreve
- To understand the difference between the sound of a semibreve and the sound of a crotchet followed by 3 beats of silence
- To develop pitch awareness

Introducing a new note value – the SEMIBREVE

> **o**
> a semibreve

- A semibreve lasts for the same length of time as 4 crotchets. Play semibreves to the children on the finger chimes. (Play these like tiny cymbals.) Count '1, 2, 3, 4' out loud and play the chimes as you say '1'. Keep the pulse absolutely even, then play another semibreve on the next number 1, and so on. Point out that each semibreve is ringing on so that it lasts for 4 crotchet beats. Ask the children to clap as you play. They should clap as you play number 1, then keep their hands together and 'pulse' their hands on numbers 2, 3, and 4. Now show what happens if you play the finger chimes wrongly (stop the bells from ringing by keeping them together). Explain to the children that these aren't proper semibreves because the sound dies straight away. The sound lasts for only 1 crotchet, followed by 3 crotchet beats of silence, instead of lasting for 4 crotchet beats.

Equal claps around the circle

- This time each child should clap a semibreve. To do this, they should only clap once then keep their hands together and pulse on 2, 3, 4 to make it a full semibreve. You play crotchets on the claves throughout to make sure that each child counts a full 4 crotchet beats for each semibreve. Whisper the counts 2, 3, 4 to be sure that these silent counts aren't rushed.

Singing and growing

- Do this activity a few times. Make sure the children aren't rushing the movements.

Copying three sounds with voice and hand signals

- Revise this activity.

The pitch game

- This is a new game. Play either G F E D C (i.e. going down to DO) or C D E F G (i.e. going up to SO) on the xylophone. The children must listen but not look. If they think you went *up* to SO, they must go to an allocated place in the room. It they think you went *down* to DO, they must go to another allocated place. Be sure to check that the children are quite clear on which places are representing DO and SO. (I usually find a place beginning with 'd' to be the DO place – e.g. door, and similarly for the SO place.) The children who go to the wrong place are 'out'. Eliminate until there is a winner. It is surprising how difficult children find this listening exercise.

Singing: *Bazookas!* (p.76)

- With the help of the CD, track 21, finish learning *Bazookas!*

Guess the food rhythms

- Divide the class into three groups and play a game of **guess the food rhythms** from Lesson 3. If you would like to be reminded of all the different food rhythms play track 23 on the CD.

Lesson 8

Objectives:
- To memorise a more complex rhythmic sequence
- To reinforce the note value – the semibreve

Stepping a sequence

- Incorporate semibreves into the opening stepping sequence as follows: 2 semibreves, 4 minims, 8 crotchets, 16 quavers.

Equal claps around the circle

- As in Lesson 7, the children should clap semibreves while you play crotchets on the claves.
- Now choose a child to play crotchets on the claves and keep the others in time.

Singing: *Bazookas!* (p.76)

- Divide the class into three groups: group one should have finger chimes or triangles, group two, claves or wooden instruments of any sort, and group three, tambours or tambourines. Use track 22, which plays the music to the whole song through twice. Each group should play as follows:
  Verse: group one accompany with semibreves
  Chorus: group two accompany with crotchets
  Verse: group three accompany with minims
  Chorus: All three groups play their *own* note value repeatedly *together*.
- You might want to try the verse first and then press pause and continue in this way to check that the children are playing the note values correctly, before trying it all the way through.

The pitch game

- Finish with this game, which was introduced last lesson.

Lesson 9

Objectives:
- To listen to and appraise classical music
- To gain familiarity with music from another culture
- To sing more complex lyrics at a faster speed while memorising and co-ordinating actions

Stepping a sequence

- As in the last lesson. Revise the tapping and stepping sequence incorporating all four note values.

Listening: *The Nutcracker Suite* by Tchaikovsky

- Explain that this is a ballet and describe what that is. Then tell the story which I have summarised below. If it is possible to use a storybook, even better!
- There are two children in the story – Klara and her brother Fritz. It is Christmas Eve and all the guests are arriving for a grand party at their house. The children at the party open the presents. Klara's favourite present is a nutcracker in the shape of a toy soldier. Her brother snatches it from her and it drops and breaks. Klara puts it gently in her doll's cradle. Later when she's fast asleep in bed, she's woken by a noise and goes downstairs to see what it is. In the sitting room the Christmas tree is lit up and all the toys and gingerbread men are marching round the tree. In the middle of them is the Nutcracker. Then an army of mice appears, led by the fierce and terrible Mouse King. Immediately the Nutcracker takes charge of the Tin Soldiers and a battle starts. The Nutcracker and the Mouse King fight with long swords and finally the Nutcracker kills the Mouse King and all the mice run away. The Nutcracker turns into a handsome Prince. He takes Klara over the lake, through a snowstorm to the Kingdom of Sweets, where all the sweets, toys and flowers dance for her. The dances get wilder and wilder and then suddenly everything goes dark. Klara can't understand it. She's lying in her bed at home. So was it all just a dream?
- Now listen to 'March' from *The Nutcracker Suite*. This is the music for the guests arriving at the party. Let the children join in marching to this rhythmic music. They could also choose a simple repetitive crotchet, minim or semibreve and do their action at this chosen speed.

Singing: *The Giant's Garden* (music: p.78)

- This song is from the story *The Selfish Giant* by Oscar Wilde. With the help of the CD, track 24, learn the first verse. See the song for the actions. The photocopiable song sheet is at the back of the book.

Lesson 10

Objective:

- To consolidate the last lesson

Singing: *The Giant's Garden* (p.78)

- Let's start with a song for a change! With the help

of the CD, track 24, revise the first verse of *The Giant's Garden* with actions. Then learn the next verse.

Listening: *The Nutcracker Suite*

- Can the children remember the story?
- Play the track called 'March' again. The children can join in with marching or improvised actions if they want. Or they should close their eyes and imagine what all the guests look like as they arrive at the party.
- Now play 'The Dance of the Sugar Plum Fairy'. This is one of the dances that Klara watched in the Kingdom of Sweets. The music is quiet and sparkling. The celesta is the instrument that sounds high and tinkling in this music. The children should tiptoe into a space and choose an action that involves focusing on one part of the body e.g. tick-tocking the head, tapping each foot in turn, bending and straightening knees, opening and closing hands etc. After about 20 seconds of doing that action, give the children a signal to change their action to one that focuses on another part of the body. Continue to the end of the dance like this, expressing the delicate music through actions.
- 'The Russian Dance' is another dance that Klara sees in the Kingdom of Sweets. Practise the following movements which can be arranged as choreography. You may want to try them out on your own beforehand. You can do the actions in any order but only change to a different one when the music sounds as though it is starting a new musical sentence. Stand in front of the children, facing them, to try the actions through. When you feel they can manage them, put the music on and go for it!

1. Standing tall, hands on waists. Step to the right then join the other foot with a stamp. Repeat to the left and continue like this.
2. Do double steps like that to each side, and clap on the 'join' of the second step each time.
3. Arms in front, forearms one on top of the other, hop from foot to foot.
4. Kicking each leg out in front on each hop like a typical Russian dance.
5. As 3. but turning.
6. Standing tall, hands on waists. Raise right arm high, in one quick action and look up at hand. Lower to waist on next beat. Repeat with left arm and so on.

Singing: *The Giant's Garden* (p.78)

- With the help of the CD, tracks 24 and/or 25 (the backing track), finish the lesson by singing the first two verses of *The Giant's Garden*.

45

Lesson 11

Objective:
- To accompany a song with four different note values, recognising and anticipating the exact moment to start and stop playing

Singing: *The Giant's Garden* (p.78)
- Divide the class into four groups and give each group instruments. Play the CD, track 25, which gives you five play-throughs of *The Giant's Garden*:
  First play-through: the first group play quavers on the claves
  Second play-through: the second group play crotchets on the tambourines
  Third play-through: the third group play minims on the tambours
  Fourth play-through: the fourth group play semibreves on the finger chimes
  Fifth play-through: all four groups should lightly play the beat of their note value simultaneously.
- Remind the children of the food rhythms they know and ask each group to choose a different one. Play the track through again and this time the four groups should take turns clapping or playing their chosen rhythm repeatedly. On the fifth play-through, see what happens if all four groups play their rhythm at the same time. Listen carefully to each other and at the end, discuss how it went. Did any group do it particularly well? What was their secret? (Usually it is having a strong leader in the group who keeps the others together. It also takes plenty of concentration!)

Listening: *The Nutcracker Suite*
- Have another go at moving to the 'March', 'The Dance of the Sugar Plum Fairy' and 'The Russian Dance'.
- To help develop the musical skill of recognising and 'feeling' phrases or musical sentences in music, listen to 'The Chinese Dance'. In a space of their own, the children should put the palms of their hands together (praying hands). Take tiny shuffling footsteps in one direction until you hear a new musical sentence or section, then change to another direction. Join in yourself so the children can be lead by you the first time. We are not talking about an in-depth musical analysis of phrasing in the piece. The aim here is simply to focus on the fact that, like speech and prose, pieces of music are 'punctuated'. You might 'feel' the music in shorter or longer phrases and change direction more or less frequently, accordingly.

Don't worry that it is right or wrong. Bringing the children's attention to *any* change to what you might perceive as the 'next bit' in the music, is the musical exercise here.

Lesson 12

Objective:
- Consolidation

Stepping a sequence
- Choose any of the sequences you have done during this term. Stop tapping whenever you want and indicate with your hands if you want the children to make a circle or a T or C shape.

The pitch game
- Revise the preliminary SO/DO activities first – **singing and growing** and **copying three sounds with voice and hand signals**. Then play the **pitch game**.

The Nutcracker Suite, 'The Chinese Dance'
- Repeat moving to 'The Chinese Dance'.

Singing: *The Giant's Garden* (p.78)
- Learn the last three verses with track 24. Then sing through the whole song with actions using the accompaniment (track 25).

Chapter 5
Year 2, Term 2

Theme: Scary stuff!

Concept: More challenging listening games

Medium-term objectives:
- To deepen skill of aural discrimination
- To focus on sustaining rhythmic patterns and beats against other rhythmic matter

Music to listen to: *Night on the Bare Mountain* by Mussorgsky

Songs: *Mum! Mum! Quickly Come; Rats!* (from *The Pied Piper*); *In the Crocodile Pool* and your own choice of songs, if required

Resources: CD; a full range of percussion instruments; all note value cards; white/black board; CD of *Night on the Bare Mountain*; song sheets (optional)

Lesson 13

Objectives:
- To develop co-ordination, memory and rhythmic skills
- To start the concept of silence and to lead on to the crotchet rest
- To revise the concepts crescendo and diminuendo

8, 4, 2 activity
- This is a new opening activity which really develops memory and listening skills, getting the children to focus on listening and to think ahead. It is also good for co-ordination.
- Repeat each of the following actions 8 times:
    Touch heads
    Clap hands
    Pat knees
    March on the spot
- Now repeat the same actions, doing each one only 4 times. Then repeat each one 2 times, twice through.
- With the CD, track 26, do the whole of the above sequence without a break. Listen out for the accents on the piano on the CD which help indicate when to move on to the next action.

A new concept – RESTS, approached through silence
- Sit or kneel in a circle with the children. Remember Year 1, Lesson 28, when we made a thunderstorm with finger and hand taps on the floor? We're going to do something similar now. But first we are going to consider silence. All sit still, be silent, close your eyes and listen for about a minute. Discuss the sounds you heard – birds singing, traffic, footsteps in the corridor etc.
- Ask the children to imagine that when you put your hands flat on the floor in front of you, that means silence. As you *slowly* raise your hands up to head level the volume is going up, and as you *slowly* lower them again the volume is going down. So you are conducting and thereby controlling an even crescendo and diminuendo. The children must watch very carefully. As your hands leave the ground they should start whispering very softly (repeating their name, or name and address, over and over again, or counting up from a hundred works well as it makes them concentrate more!). Always watching your hands carefully and listening to the sound growing, they should build a 'words' crescendo and then, equally carefully, a diminuendo as your hands lower and the voices turn to whispers then to silence. If you are counting, make sure you count down during this! What you have just done is to leave silence *gradually* and re-enter silence *gradually*.
- Now let's leave silence gradually and this time re-enter it *suddenly*. Repeat the same word exercise, only this time, when your hands reach their highest point, lower them to the ground in one sharp movement. The children must go from talking very loudly to being silent.

47

- Now let's leave silence *suddenly* and re-enter *gradually*. Here the children are going to clap their hands rather than use their voices. The children must watch you very carefully and when you *suddenly* raise your hands from the floor, straight to eye level, they must imagine that they have been watching a spectacular show and there is a moment of silence as the final curtain comes down, before they (the audience) break into loud applause. As you *gradually* lower your hands their clapping fades into silence. This diminuendo is the most difficult to judge – encourage the children not to clap too quietly too soon.

- The above activities exploring silence lend weight to the idea that silence is something positive. When little silences happen within a piece of music they are there for a reason – to strengthen the quality of the music in some way.

The crotchet rest

- Short silences in music are called RESTS. We are going to deal with a rest that lasts for one crotchet beat. Show the children what the crotchet rest looks like.

Demonstrating ♩ ♩ 𝄽 ♩

- Now have four children at the front, each holding one **crotchet** card. The other children should clap and count from 1 to 4 as you point to each **crotchet** card. 'What number is Tom?' 'Yes, number 3.' Take Tom's **crotchet** card and give him a card with a **crotchet rest**. This time when the children clap and count from 1 to 4, they should make the third count a silent count, mouthing the word 3, while turning their palms up (empty = empty of sound). Swap the crotchet rest to the second then fourth count and clap these examples through. Now try some examples substituting more notes with crotchet rests. It is best to count once through to 4 at the same speed as you intend to clap *before* you start clapping, especially where you need to lead into a rest on the first count.

Copying three sounds with voice and hand signals

- Revise SO and DO through this activity then play a game of running to the allocated area for each one.

Singing: *Mum! Mum! Quickly Come* (music: p.80)

- With the help of the CD, track 27, learn the chorus of *Mum! Mum! Quickly Come*. The photocopiable song sheet is at the back of the book.

Lesson 14

Objectives:

- To deepen the understanding of rests
- To introduce a new pitched sound – MI

8, 4, 2

- Start with this activity.

Revising the crotchet rest

- With four children standing in a row at the front, clap a combination of crotchets and rests. Some examples are below:

- Ask another child if they can give the right card to the right child to represent what you have just clapped. Now ask the four children themselves to listen carefully to what you clap. If you clap

48

then the first and third children should remain standing while the second and fourth children sit down. Continue trying out combinations of crotchets and rests with other groups of four children.

- Now divide the whole class into rows of four and clap various examples as before. The first team (each row is a team) to arrange themselves correctly gets a point. The first team to gain three points, wins!

Introducing a new pitched sound – MI

- Play C E G on the xylophone. The note in the middle of DO and SO is called MI (pronounced ME) The hand signal is:

MI

Now try **copying three sounds with voice and hand signals** using all three known pitched notes.

Singing: *Mum! Mum! Quickly Come*

- With the help of the CD, track 27, revise the chorus of *Mum! Mum! Quickly Come*, then learn the first two verses.

Lesson 15

Objectives:

- To revise the four note values
- To consolidate rests
- To sustain a rhythmic pattern against (up to) three others

Extended magic cards 3

- Start with a game of **magic cards** for a change.

Look back to Year 1, Lesson 35. Here the children had to gradually form three groups of *like* cards, (**minims**, **crotchets** and **quavers**), by clapping the note value on their card and watching the others clapping. After reminding the children of how to play the game (see Year 1, Lesson 33), play it in the same way now but incorporate semibreves so the children have to form four groups. You should always play a steady crotchet beat on the drum to keep everyone together.

Consolidating crotchet rests

- Copy the following onto the board:

- The vertical lines separating each group of 4 beats are called bar lines and make the music visually easier to follow. So in 4-time each group of 4 beats forms one bar.
- The whole class should practise clapping each row of rhythms.
- Now give each row an animal sound, such as 'quack' or 'moo'. Again, the whole class should try each row out, this time saying the rhythm with the animal sounds instead of clapping.
- Now divide the class into two halves. One half does the first rhythm to 'quack' the other half does the second rhythm to 'moo'.
- Next divide the class into three groups, introducing a third animal sound for the third row of notes and rests, and trying all three groups together. Finally try with all four rhythms. To help them, point to one of the rows on the board. You can't point to all four at once obviously, so I usually point to the most difficult one. Check that the balance of sounds is good and adjust the number of children in the groups accordingly. (Or you might have to transfer a loud child to a quiet group!)

Singing: *Mum! Mum! Quickly Come* (p.80)

- With the help of track 27 revise the first two verses and the chorus of *Mum! Mum! Quickly Come* and then learn verse three.

Lesson 16

Objectives:
- To develop rhythmic discrimination
- Further consolidation of the pitched sounds DO, MI and SO

Extended magic cards 3
- Use all four note values.

The code game
- We are going to play a game of **if it's your name, run!** as we did in Year 1, Lesson 34, but with a slight variation, so the game is re-titled the **code game.** The extension here is that you are identifying one specific child. You will need a drum, a tambourine and a pair of claves.
- Ask the children to think about the sounds of their name and to work out whose names in the class sound the same. (Have a class name list in front of you and work this out for yourself in advance.) With your help the children should arrange themselves in pairs or groups according to the sounds of their names. Some children might be in a group of only two, others of five or six and a few children will be alone. The children in pairs should number themselves 1 and 2. Those in groups should number themselves 1, 2, 3 etc and remember their number.
- With the class list in front of you, and the children remaining in the groups they have just formed, play the rhythm of any child's name on the **drum**. At this stage the children are trying to recognise if this is the right sound for *their name*.
- If you have played the name of a child who is in a pair or a group, those children need to know exactly which child you have in mind. So next you should play the **tambourine** to give them another clue as to the name you are playing. If you play, for example, 1 tap it signifies the first person of the group/pair, 2 taps signifies the second, 4 taps will mean the fourth person (so this would mean someone from a larger group) and so on. If you don't play *any* taps then the children will have the added clue that it must be one of those children sitting on their own.
- Finally the **claves** tells the selected child *where* to run by tapping the number of syllables in the word – 1 tap for door etc. You can play up to 5 taps. You don't have to struggle to find a word with five syllables in your room – you could have, for example, 'Lots of coloured balls' which has five syllables. You will only have time for a few

examples but there are plenty more opportunities to play this during the term.

The pitch game, incorporating MI
- Run through some examples of SO, MI, DO with hand signals.
- Now play the **pitch game** incorporating MI. As before, you can finish on DO, playing G F E D C or you can finish on SO playing C D E F G. The new one here is to finish on MI by playing either G F E D E or C D E F E. As before, the children should be aware of the allocated places in the room for DO and SO. Establish that for MI, they should stay in the middle, stand up and put hands on waists.

Singing: *Mum! Mum! Quickly Come* (p.80)
- With the help of track 27, finish the lesson learning the whole song.

Lesson 17

Objectives:
- To work on the skill of co-operation to facilitate group work
- To work on crotchets and rests with particular focus on anticipation and co-ordination skills

The code game
- Start with a few examples of this.

Starting to work in groups
- From this point onwards children might be required to work on their own in groups. I find it worthwhile spending a bit of time establishing good principles for this kind of group work.
- Divide the class into five or six groups. Each group should sit in a small circle. Explain to the class that you're going to see which group is best at agreeing with each other. If you say *colour* then each group must choose one colour and sit quietly watching you. When you point to a group, the whole group must call out their chosen colour *at the same time*. If you say *furniture*, they might choose table or bookcase. If you say *place*, they might choose home, school, London, Manchester or Africa – anything goes! Explain that if you point to one group and the children in that group call out different things from each other, then it shows that the group hasn't agreed very well. If someone in the group doesn't say anything, that's no good either. Everyone must call out the same

thing at the same time to show that the group have decided quickly and agreed together.

- Children love this game and whenever you want to do group work in the future in any subject, if you remind them of this activity it should help increase the co-operation factor!

Clapping on different beats ***

- This is a new rhythmic exercise. Here we are going to clap a series of rhythms made up of 1 crotchet and 3 crotchet rests in different combinations.
- Start tapping 4 crotchet beats on any note of the xylophone. Tap loudly on beat 1, then tap very softly on beats 2, 3 and 4. The loud beats that you are playing represent the crotchet beats and the quiet beats represent the crotchet rests. Stick to the same note and keep repeating this pattern while the children join in clapping on beat 1 and showing the 3 rests for the other 3 beats by turning their palms up. It is helpful to say, 'Count number 1 loudly and 2, 3, and 4 quietly'.
- Now change to a different xylophone note and establish a pattern where your loud tap is on beat 2 and the other three are much quieter. Say, 'Count number 2 loudly, and numbers 1, 3 and 4 quietly'. The children clap accordingly.
- Then with another xylophone note, establish a pattern where you tap loudly on beat 3, and the children clap and count accordingly, and finally with another note, on beat 4.
- Now tell the children you are going to do *four* run-throughs of each pattern without a break, and therefore they must clap and count without a break. This means concentrating hard and thinking ahead.
- If the children can do this easily, try doing just *two* run-throughs of each pattern. Then go back to the start without a break and do another two run-throughs and so on. Moving from one set of two to the next is quite tricky!
- Finally try with just *one* run-through of each – even trickier! This is how it will sound:

Singing: *Mum! Mum! Quickly Come* (p.80)

- Use the CD, track 28. Divide the class into five groups and let the groups take turns to sing a verse each. All join in singing the chorus.

Objective:

■ To learn two new food rhythms and incorporate them with the others

8, 4, 2

- Warm up with this activity.

The code game

- Have a few games of this.

Learning two new food rhythms

- For each of these, have four children in a row in front of the other children. For HAM ROLL, give the first and third children a **minim** card. The second and fourth children have nothing because each minim lasts for 2 counts. For HAM SANDWICH, the first child should hold a **minim**, the second child, nothing, and the third and fourth children should both hold **crotchets**. Clap through these rhythms.

Responding to food rhythms in groups

- This was first learnt in Year 1, Lesson 29, where it was played in groups of four and then in Lesson 36 where it was played in groups of six. Play it here incorporating the two new food rhythms.

Singing: *Mum! Mum! Quickly Come* (p.80)

- Sing this all the way through with the accompaniment on track 28.

Objectives:

■ To learn a new food rhythm and incorporate it with the others
■ To develop rhythmic skills with the introduction of the new concept, CANON

The code game

- To warm up.

Learning a new food rhythm

MAR-MA-LADE   SAND - WICH

- Check that the children can remember the two new rhythms from the last lesson.
- With four children at the front of the class, demonstrate and learn the new food rhythm MARMALADE SANDWICH. The first child holds a **quaver** card while the last three hold a **crotchet** card each.
- Now divide the class into five groups. Each group must agree on a food rhythm, without letting the other groups hear!
- Each group then takes turns to clap their food rhythm four times through without a break, taking care not to mouth it as they clap! Can anyone from another group say what it is? The more easily a rhythm was guessed, the more clearly it was clapped.

Starting a new concept – CANON

- You might have heard of singing 'in a round' – songs such as *Frère Jacques* are sung 'in a round'. The proper musical name for this is singing in CANON. This requires a very good sense of pitch and of rhythm. In this activity we are going to develop the rhythmic side of this by aurally being aware of two different things going on at the same time. This is a great life skill.
- **Clapping in canon**. Reaching your hands out to the right hand side, clap and say EGGS AND BACON, then above your head, clap and say HAM ROLL, then reaching out to the left side, clap and say SAUSAGES AND BREAD AND BUTTER, then pat your knees and say TOAD IN THE HOLE. At first the children should try the sequence *with* you, then they should do it in canon. You start first, and when you have done EGGS AND BACON they start the sequence with EGGS AND BACON, while you move on to HAM ROLL. Continue like this, so the children are always exactly one food rhythm behind you.
- **Action Canon**: The children should stand in two rows slightly more than a metre apart facing each other. First learn the following action sequence together:
4 claps
4 nods
4 knee pats
4 marches (on the spot)
4 short moves to get down to a crouching position
4 short moves to get back up again

4 steps forward
4 steps back

- Now try it in canon. For this, the second row should begin the sequence when the first row have done their 4 claps. You maintain a steady crotchet beat on the drum throughout to keep everyone in time.

Singing: *Rats!* (music: p.82)

- With the help of the CD, track 29, start to learn the song *Rats!* The greater part of this song is in canon. Divide the class into two parts and listen carefully! The photocopiable song sheet is at the back of the book.

Lesson 20

Objectives:
- To consolidate and extend the canon work
- To learn a new food rhythm

Consolidating the canon work

- Start with the action canon in two rows, then try the same thing in four rows. The four rows should be arranged to form the sides of a square with all the children facing inwards. Each row should begin the sequence 4 beats (claps) later than the row before them. Again play a steady beat on the drum to keep everyone in time.

A new food rhythm

MAR-MA-LADE   ROLL

- Revise HAM ROLL, HAM SANDWICH and MARMALADE SANDWICH, then learn MARMALADE ROLL in the usual way.
- Divide the class into six groups. Give each group cards for a food rhythm making sure at least two of the new ones are included.
- Put on the CD, track 30, which is two play-throughs of the music for *Twinkle, Twinkle Little Star* (without vocals). There is a brief introduction then the music starts. The first group must play their food rhythm twice, in time with the CD track and without a break, the second group should play theirs twice, then the third group, and so on. Repeat this sequence.

Singing: *Rats!* (p.82)

- Have another go at this song with the CD, track 29. Then try it using track 31 which is the accompaniment only.

The pitch game

- Finish with this if you have time.

Lesson 21

Objectives:

- To learn a new food rhythm
- To extend the canon work

Stepping a sequence

- Start with this activity for a change. For a reminder, look back to Year 2, Lesson 1 and 8.

Learning a new food rhythm

IC - ING ON CHOC-'LATE CAKE

- Learn the rhythm in the usual way. Make sure the children understand this rhythm. (I once asked a class to identify the rhythm, and got the answer, '*We* sing on chocolate cake.' That's when I realised that they might not have grasped that we were talking about '*icing*' here and not '*I sing*'!)

Working in Canon

- Repeat the canon activities from Lessons 19 and 20 and then try this stepping activity. Play on the drum EGGS AND BACON twice, SAUSAGES AND BREAD AND BUTTER twice, EGGS AND BACON twice, HAM ROLL twice. The children can try stepping the sequence once through at the same time as your drum beat, then they should try it in canon with your drum beat.

The pitch game

- Have a few games of this.

Singing: *Rats!* (p.82)

- If required, use track 31 which is the accompaniment only.

Lesson 22

Objective:

- To listen to and appraise music from another culture

Listening: *Night on the Bare Mountain* by Mussorgsky

- **Background information:** This is a composition arranged and orchestrated by Rimsky-Korsakov. He took the passage from part of a composition by another composer – Mussorgsky. It is wonderfully evocative music which the children will love.
- The original story talks of witches, werewolves and the like, revelling at a Midsummer Night's Party. This is their great annual festival and they are celebrating the end of the long days and the beginning of the long nights, where they can come into their own! I have toned down the story (below) to make it more appropriate for young children. However, you might prefer to make up your own story. After all, there is no rule that you have to stick rigidly to any particular storyline. I feel that the story serves a purpose as the 'attention grabber' to bring the music to life, so as long as you are not suggesting that a lullaby is a mad stampede of wild elephants or some such, you can be as creative as you want!
- Before you play the music, tell the children the story below in your own words.
  The story: A lone traveller comes across a desolate-looking mountain that he knows must be crossed in order to reach the village on the other side. When the traveller reaches the top of the mountain he looks down, and sure enough there is a pretty little village laid out below. He decides to have a rest before continuing. He is quite sure that there is plenty of time to reach the village before it gets dark. When he awakes however, he is shocked to find that it is already pitch black, and the air around him feels cold and scary. From the sky above, there comes a strange blue light whizzing and spinning through the darkness. When it settles on the highest peak, it turns out to be the chief monster with glittering eyes and enormous wings. The traveller hides in a crevice on the mountainside as ear splitting noises fill the air and all sorts of scary creatures – monsters and goblins – descend upon the mountain as if from nowhere. The creatures have met on the mountain top to have a party because they like going out in the dark to scare each other! At the end of the music, the church bells in the village ring out to say that dawn is breaking. The

moment the creatures hear the bells, they fly away terrified because they know that daylight is coming.

- **Now play the music:** While listening to the music, pause the CD every so often to discuss what might be happening 'in that bit'. The creatures might be dancing, or tiptoeing up on each other, trying to scare one another. Or it might be music which suggests the wind hanging around the mountain like heavy smelly curtains, or it might suggest the traveller's fear as he tries to tuck himself deeper into a crevice so as not to be seen. When the music sounds imperious and authoritative this could be the chief monster spreading his wings to make everyone stop talking, drinking and eating, and listen to him. You might be able to picture a magic fire blazing in the centre of the party. Maybe the creatures hurl their empty beakers into the flames and make the smoke change colour as it billows into the dark sky. The bells of dawn are slow and calm after all the excitement, and the harp represents the first rays of sun glinting on the mountain. This conclusion, in stark contrast to the earlier music, is reminiscent of *The Sorcerer's Apprentice* which also finished with a 'thank-goodness-for-that' feel!

- **Follow up:** The music inspires English and art work, because children's imaginations can be let loose describing the nasty creatures, the contrasting emotions of the traveller to those of the creatures, and of the excitement to the subsequent calm; as well as the atmosphere – the sight, smell, sound and feel of the darkness and dankness. If you can find any pictures which illustrate this story or parts of the story, then feel free to use them as these will enhance the listening experience for the children.

Singing: *In the Crocodile Pool* (music: p.83)

- Learn this new song with the help of the CD, track 32. All three verses are the same, apart from the names of the crocodiles, which change each time.

Objective:

- To feel the mood and atmosphere of a piece of classical music and to interpret it with free movement

8, 4, 2

- Start with this activity for a change!

Singing: *In the Crocodile Pool* (p.83)

- Using the CD, track 32, continue to learn this song. Can the children recognise the rhythm TOAD IN THE HOLE in the words 'Don't want to see', which come twice, near to the end of each verse?

- Now divide the class into three groups, and give each group percussion instruments so you have three sets of contrasting sounds. Then each group must choose its own food rhythm, find the right cards for this rhythm, and set them out in front of them. Go around the groups and check that they all have a rhythm before you start.

- Play the music again, and after the introduction, the three groups take turns to play their chosen rhythm twice. When all the groups have played, repeat once through. For the last two bars of the music and the introduction to the next verse, the three groups should move round one place and quickly work out what rhythm they must play this time. The initial order in which the three rhythms are played should remain the same for each verse, so it won't be the same group of children who play first each time. As there are three verses, each group gets to play all three rhythms.

Listening: *Night on the Bare Mountain*

- **Improvised movement:** Remind the children of the imaginative pictures that the music to *Night on the Bare Mountain* conjured up during the last lesson. Now you are going to try some improvised movement. Play some extracts of the music – each one under a minute in duration – and ask the children to move freely. They might want to pretend to be one of the monsters, for example. Encourage them to simply let their bodies *be* the music and express themselves freely and clearly. Ask them to imagine that they are trying to show a deaf person in the room exactly what the music sounds like by the way they move. The children must try to convey the feelings in the music through sharp, pointed, kicking movements, or low, creeping bent movements, or big leaps and wide stretched movements. Sometimes move on the spot and sometimes move around. Not all children feel comfortable moving like this but as long as they are 'involved' in the music, it doesn't matter if they are moving or not.

Clapping on different beats
- Finish with this activity from Lesson 17.

Lesson 24

Objective:
■ To create a whole-class percussion piece, recording the piece and appraising it critically

Opening activity
- Start with an activity of your choice, e.g. **signals**.

Creating a whole-class improvisation/composition using percussion
- Sit in a circle with a wide selection of percussion instruments in front of you. Talk about *Night on the Bare Mountain*. You are going to try and create your own piece based on this story, just as Rimsky-Korsakov created his piece based on something that Mussorgsky had written. Your piece should fall somewhere between a composition and an improvisation.
- Talk with the children about how the music should start and finish. Consider how they will know when to play. Bring yourself in as a conductor here. As long as the children remember to keep an eye on you at all times, you can signal to them in any way you want to get effects. Talk about whether all the children should always play all the time, or whether solos, or small groups of sound would be appropriate. Think about which sounds will create which effects. Talk about the emotion of the music and try out some ideas. Remember the entering and leaving silence activities you did which incorporated crescendo and diminuendo. Can you include silence in your piece?
- Your piece shouldn't be more than 2 minutes long. When you have decided upon a rough 'outline' go for it!
- When it is finished – and be sure that you have planned the very end, otherwise it will go on and on forever! – discuss its merits and its bad points, and try again. By the third time, it should sound

pretty good. How about recording it and listening to it critically. Then try it again. Practice makes perfect!

Singing: *In the Crocodile Pool* (p.83)
- Use track 33 (accompaniment).

Chapter 6
Year 2, Term 3

Theme: Feelings

Concept: Working out 4-time rhythms by counting instead of using food words

Medium-term objective:
- To consolidate and extend work in all areas of the subject

Music to listen to: Revisiting *Carnival of the Animals* by Saint-Saëns

Songs: *I'm Sorry*; *The Grand Old Duke Of York*; *What Annie McRae Wanted For Tea*; *Technology Grind*

Resources: CD; a whole range of percussion instruments; all contrast cards; all note value cards; black/white board; CD of *Carnival of the Animals*; song sheets (optional)

Lesson 25

Objective:
- To focus on counting and internalisation
- To be aware of instrumentation

Additional resource: contrasts cards

A new opening activity – stepping and stopping

- First remind the children of the discussion and activities which have taken place in connection with silence and rests.
- This is a tricky counting exercise which needs great concentration. You are going to keep the children in time by playing a very quiet beat on the drum. At first, play every single beat, whether a crotchet or a rest, on your drum, tapping the rests much more quietly than the crotchets. The children should *only* take steps on the crotchets. They should stand still on the rests and count them in their heads.
- Keeping a regular beat inside your head is much more difficult than maintaining it while playing an instrument or doing actions. It is called INTERNALISATION and is an important musical skill. How the children should step is laid out below. It rolls on without a break.

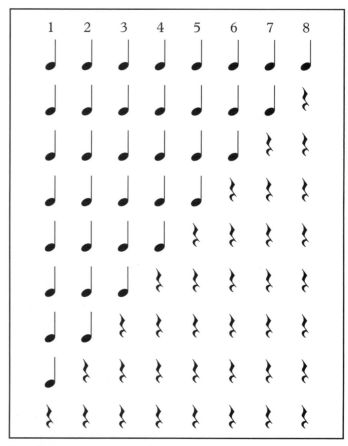

Random contrasts cards

- Refer back to Year 1, Lesson 10. You will remember the game using the **contrasts cards** in teams. The children had to listen to a piece of music such as 'The Aviary' (from *Carnival of the Animals*) and then hold up the card which describes that music. Now for an extension, **random contrasts cards**.
- Divide the class into teams of four. Each team should arrange itself in a row. You need one set of

56

8 cards per team. Shuffle each set and hand out the 8 cards at random, so that each member of the team gets 2 cards. They won't necessarily be contrasts like **frog** and **snake**. One child might get the **galloping horse** (fast) and the **soldier** (loud) for example. Using the CD, track 34 play the first extract. The children should all listen and look at their cards. They should then display one, both or neither of their cards, according to what the music sounds like. The first example is Loud, Slow, Jumpy and High. Whichever team displays the correct 4 cards (**soldier**, **tortoise**, **frog** and **bird**) gains a point.

- There are six short extracts on track 34, with pauses in between. You will need to pause the CD immediately after each extract to see how the children have done before moving onto the next extract. The answers and CD timings are below:
  1. Loud, Slow, Jumpy, High
  2. High, Quiet, Fast, Smooth   (0.17)
  3. Low, Loud, Fast, Smooth   (0.35)
  4. Low, Quiet, Fast, Jumpy   (0.51)
  5. High, Quiet, Slow, Jumpy   (1.07)
  6. Low, Loud, Slow, Smooth   (1.25)

Singing: *I'm Sorry* (music: p.84)

- With the help of the CD, track 35, learn verse one and the chorus of *I'm Sorry*. The photocopiable song sheet is at the back of the book.

Starting to revisit *Carnival of the Animals*

- This term we are going to tackle all 14 sections of *Carnival of the Animals*. Much of it will be revision and some parts will be brand new. First explain to the children that Saint-Saëns wrote this music as a joke. I will say more about that with specific examples as they come up. The orchestral arrangement is unusual because it is written for the odd combination of two pianos, two violins, viola, cello, double bass, flute, clarinet, celesta and xylophone. A celesta looks like a mini piano, but instead of having strings inside it, it has rows of steel bars which make a sound like bells when they are struck. The celesta is also used in 'The Dance of the Sugar Plum Fairy' from *The Nutcracker Suite*, which we listened to in Year 2, Term 1.
- Finish by revisiting 'The Royal March of the Lion', which is written for strings and two pianos. Listen to the lions waking up at the start of the music, then join in marching when the lions march. Listen out for the 'growls' on the two pianos.

Objective:
- To begin to work out rhythms by counting rather than using food words

Stepping and stopping

Singing: *I'm Sorry* (p.84)

- With the help of the CD, track 35, revise the first verse and chorus of *I'm Sorry* then learn verse two.

Rhythm building without food words

- A turning point has come! From this moment onwards the children are going to dispense with their food words, and learn how to build up any combination of the known note values to create all sorts of rhythms in 4-time. You could liken this process to dispensing with letter sounds and referring to letter names.
- Have four children standing side by side, in front of the others. Give each child a **crotchet** card and count and clap from 1 to 4 as you point to each card in order.
- Now remove the **crotchet** card from the third child and give them a **quaver** card. Tell the children that whenever they see 2 quavers, the second one is the magic word 'and'. The crotchets are plain numbers. So you count and clap this rhythm as follows:

This rhythm is the first example to appear on the CD, track 36. While listening to this track, try clapping this first one yourself beforehand to be absolutely sure you're not saying the 'and' too soon after the number 3.

- Now give the second child the **quaver** card, and the others the crotchets. Clap and count this rhythm:

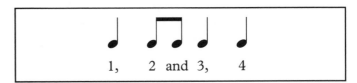

This is the second example on track 36.

- Now give the fourth child the **quaver** card and

57

give the other children crotchets. All clap and count '1, 2, 3, 4 and'. The danger here is that the children instinctively want to say the 'and' *before* the 4. So be careful with this one! It is the third example on track 36.

- Finally give the first child the **quaver** card. All clap and count '1 and, 2, 3, 4'. This is the fourth example on track 36.

- Now you are going to use the whole of track 36. The rhythms are written out in order below. Each rhythm is played by the piano on this track and you must simply repeat it in the pause before the next one. This pause is exactly the right length of time for you and the class to clap back the rhythm. You will notice that there are rhythms with more than one pair of quavers included. When you have done all 8 examples, re-play the track and pause the CD after you have heard each one; see if the children can tell you how to write it up on the board.

Listening: *Carnival of the Animals*

- Listen to the piece 'Cocks and Hens', which is very short. This is played by a clarinet, two pianos, violins and viola. Imagine the cocks and hens cackling, strutting, scrabbling around in the dirt for food and 'cock-a-doodle-dooing'!

Objective:
- Reinforcement

Stepping and stopping

- Try this activity the other way round. So start with stepping on count number 1 and standing still and counting from 2 to 8, then step on counts 1 and 2, and stand still and count from 3 to 8, etc. See the diagram below:

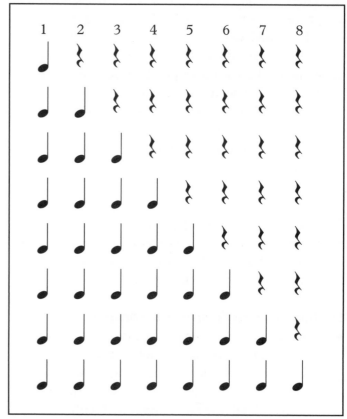

Random contrasts cards

- Using the CD, track 37, try these six further examples in teams of four as in Lesson 25. There are pauses in between each one on the CD track. Below are the answers:
  1. High, Quiet, Slow, Smooth
  2. Low, Quiet, Slow, Jumpy   (0.22)
  3. High, Loud, Fast, Jumpy   (0.42)
  4. Low, Quiet, Fast, Smooth   (0.58)
  5. High, Loud, Slow, Smooth   (1.19)
  6. Low, Loud, Fast, Jumpy   (1.42)

Singing: *I'm Sorry* (p.84)

- Learn the third verse of the song *I'm Sorry* with the CD, track 35. Divide the class into three groups – one to sing each verse. All join in with the chorus each time. Try singing it through with track 38, which is the accompaniment only.

Year 2
Term 3

Listening: 'Wild Asses' from *Carnival of the Animals*

- Listen to the piece entitled 'Wild Asses' and hear how the music races up and down on two pianos.

Lesson 28

Objectives:

- Reinforcement
- To learn a new note value – the dotted minim

Stepping and stopping

- Repeat this exercise the way you did it in the previous lesson.

Working on rhythm building without food words

- Look back to **revising the crotchet rest** in Year 2, Lesson 14. We are going to play a team game like this. Arrange the whole class into rows of four. The only difference is that here we are using quavers instead of rests. Clap a combination of crotchets and quavers. The first team to arrange itself correctly according to what you have just clapped, gains a point. Just as sitting down indicated a rest in the previous version of this game, so hands on heads indicates a pair of quavers here.

Showing ♩ ♩ ♫ ♩

Listening: *Carnival of the Animals*

- Listen to 'The Tortoise'. This is written for the piano and the strings. Remember the Can-Can joke? (see Year 1, Lesson 8).
- Now listen to 'The Elephant', which is written for the piano and double bass. This is a very famous solo for the double bass, because normally double basses don't have their own melodies to play. Listen out for the tinkling piano music, which reminds us of fairies dancing. The joke here is that Saint-Saëns has contrasted a big lumbering elephant trying to waltz around, with delicate little fairies dancing. This music is in 3-time. Try clapping in 3-time with the music. Do this by clapping on the strong beat each time, which will be number 1. Then pulse your hands on beats 2 and 3.

Learning a new note value – the DOTTED MINIM

- Show the **dotted minim** card and explain that this note lasts for 3 counts because the minim is worth 2 and the dot is worth 1. Have four children stand up at the front, side by side, facing the rest of the class. Give the first one a **dotted minim** card and the last one a **crotchet** card. Do the children understand why the middle two children cannot have a card if the first one has a dotted minim? Clap this rhythm a few times without a break.

Singing: *I'm Sorry* (p.84)

- Sing the song through with the CD, track 38.

Lesson 29

Objective:

- To continue to work on understanding rhythms by counting, incorporating the dotted minim

Stepping and stopping

- Try incorporating the two versions of **stepping and stopping** into one exercise. Start with 8 steps, and then 7, 6 etc (as in Lesson 25). When the children have only stepped on 1 and counted from 2 – 8, they should show 8 beats of silence by being still. Then go on to the second version and start counting up again (as in Lesson 27).

Rhythm building with the team game

- We are going to play a team game as in the last lesson, only this time you might incorporate minims and/or dotted minims into your rhythm. For a minim, two children hold hands, and for a dotted minim, three children hold hands.

Teams demonstrating ♩ ♫ ♫

- Below are a number of possible rhythms that you could clap. Try them all out carefully before you start the game. It is important that you are quite clear yourself how to clap them, before you begin.

Listening: *Carnival of the Animals*

- Listen to 'The Kangaroo'. This is written for two pianos. Notice the hopping at the start followed by slower jumping.
- Now listen to 'The Aquarium'. This is written for two pianos, flute, celesta, violins, viola and cello. Remind the children what a celesta is (see Lesson 25). Imagine all the different coloured fishes darting in the aquarium, flicking their tails and sending bubbles up. This is shimmery, rippling music. How many different actions can they find to do with their fingers, hands, wrists, elbows and whole arms which relate to the images the music inspires?

Lesson 30

Objectives:
- To work on internalisation
- To begin to recognise the difference between counting in 2s, in 3s and in 4s

Singing
- Start by singing a well known song such as *The Grand Old Duke Of York*.
- Next, talk about what happens when you switch off the radio in the middle of a song. If you switched the radio back on again a few seconds later, would it still be on the same bit or would the song have moved on?
- Pretend to 'switch the radio on' (with an appropriate hand signal). The children should start singing *The Grand Old Duke Of York*, and when you 'switch the radio off' (with a different signal) they must instantly stop singing but *carry on inside their heads*. When you 'switch the radio back on' again, they should continue singing out loud from where they are up to inside their heads. You may have to sing the song through a few times without a break (i.e. mixing the singing *and* the silent singing as though it is all sung out loud) to get enough examples of this. This is another way of developing the skill of internalisation and can be applied to any song at any time.

Understanding metre – 3-time and 4-time
- We are used to counting in 4s (all the food rhythms) and have begun to count in 3s (with 'The Elephant'). If you are listening to a piece of music and you find that it fits when you clap in 4s, you say that the music is in 4-time or has a 4-time metre. If clapping in 3's fits the music, it

60

is in 3-time or has a 3-time metre. Have a brief discussion about this.

A new exercise – stepping and clapping the metre***

- The following exercise needs a great deal of concentration and co-ordination. In this lesson we are only going to consider the 4-time metre.
- Play repeated crotchets on a low note of your xylophone with one beater, counting in 4s. At the same time with another beater, play a high note on the first beat of each set of 4. Try it out before the lesson. The other thing you have to be able to do is swap these two parts, so you play the 4 crotchets at the top of the xylophone and the first note of each set of 4 at the bottom. You can make the change whenever you want, and then after a bit, swap back!
- Now tell the children to step round the room keeping in time with your low crotchet beat and to be aware that this low note represents what their feet are doing. Then start introducing the high note at the same time. This high note is representing the children's hands clapping. So they are doing 1 clap to every 4 steps, and when you swap, they must swap too. So they will be stepping only 1 step to every 4 claps.

Singing: *What Annie McRae Wanted For Tea*
(music: p.86)

- With the help of the CD, track 39, learn the first chorus and verse of *What Annie McRae Wanted For Tea*. The photocopiable song sheet is at the back of the book.

Listening: *Carnival of the Animals*

- Listen to the short piece, 'People With Long Ears' (Saint-Saëns' joke about donkeys!). There is just one violin making the 'hee-haw' sound of a donkey.
- Now let the children lie down and close their eyes to listen to 'The Cuckoo in the Woods'. Two pianos suggest the tall shady trees and the clarinet plays the cuckoos. Can the children concentrate for long enough to count how many cuckoos there are altogether? They should count in their heads. You'll be surprised how few get it right! (There are 21 of them.)

Lesson 31

Objectives:

- To develop an understanding and feel of the differences between 2-time, 3-time and 4-time metre
- To be able to isolate specific sounds amongst a mass of sounds

Additional resource: Cards with the names of four different sorts of animals written on them. You will need enough for the class to have one each

Singing: *What Annie McRae Wanted For Tea* (p.86)

- With the help of the CD, track 39, learn the chorus and verse two of this song.

Stepping and clapping the metre

- First go over what you did last time. Now try the same exercise but in 3-time. You will start by playing 3 crotchets on a low note of the xylophone whilst playing a high note once on the first crotchet of each set of 3. Repeat this. Then try this in 2-time, playing your high note once against each set of 2 crotchets. It is a good idea for half the children to watch the other half to see how they are getting on.

Listening: *Carnival of the Animals*

- Listen to 'The Aviary'. This is for the flute, two pianos and strings. Imagine magic birds flying about and chirping. This piece of music has a wonderful shimmery, mysterious feel to it.

Collecting animal noises

- This new game will help you and the children to focus on specific sounds. You will need four leaders. Whisper the name of an animal to each one – cat, mouse, dog, cow – and give them a corner each. They must remember their animal. These leaders are going to 'collect' the children who are making the noise of the animal you whispered to them. Give the remaining children a card each, on which is written the name of the animal whose noise they are about to make. They should sit in a space and when you say 'Go!', all start making their noise loudly. The four leaders move amongst them listening for the noise of their animal in the cacophony. When they hear it, they should take the child who is making that noise to their corner and go back to find another one. Once in the corner, the children should be silent and keep their card hidden. If there are 24 children in the class the winning team will be the one whose leader is first to collect five children making the right animal noise. Check the cards at the very end.

Collecting note values

- This is an extension of the previous game.
- Give out equal numbers of cards with crotchets, semibreves, minims and quavers on them. This time the four leaders are collecting one category of note value by listening to the children clapping their given note value. As with **extended magic cards** from Year 1, Lesson 33, you keep the beat by playing crotchets on a drum.

Lesson 32

Objectives:

- To deepen the understanding and feel of the difference between the three metres
- To develop co-ordination skills
- To consolidate the skill of identifying a specific sound in a mass of sounds

Singing: *What Annie McRae Wanted For Tea* (p.86)

- With the help of the CD, track 39, learn the third chorus and verse of this song.

Stepping and clapping the metre – an extension

- The CD, track 40 provides a further extension to this exercise. Here the three metres are mixed up randomly so the children will need to swap what their hands and feet are doing at any time. Remind them that high notes represent hands clapping and low notes represent the feet. Try it through more than once. There is no pause between time signatures on the track – one rolls into the next. If this is version is too demanding just stick to the original one.

Listening: *Carnival of the Animals*

- Listen to the piece called 'Pianists'. This is for two pianos and strings. Again Saint-Saëns is joking. He thinks pianists are like animals in the way they practise their scales up and down, up and down, all the time! The loud string chords are supposed to be the gruff voices of the piano teachers! You might notice a few deliberate 'wrong notes' in this piece.

Collecting note values

- Finish with a game of this.

Lesson 33

Objective:

- To continue to work on understanding rhythms by counting, with the focus on the 3-time metre

An activity of your choice

- Just to warm you up.

Rhythm building with the team game in 3-time

- We are going to play a team game as in Lesson 29, but instead of the children being in teams of four, representing one bar in 4-time (one lot of 4), they should stand side by side in teams of six, representing two bars in 3-time (two lots of 3). Leave a little gap between the third and fourth children to show clearly the division between the two lots of 3. Play the game in the same way, where *you* clap a rhythm from the examples below, and the children must arrange themselves accordingly. The first team to do that gains a point.

Year 2
Term 3

Listening: 'Fossils' from *Carnival of the Animals*

- 'Fossils' is a piece written for clarinet, xylophone, piano and strings. First just listen and try to identify the various instruments. Notice how the clarinet goes from very high to very low at the end of the piece. The joke here is that fossils are old bones and Saint-Saëns is using old tunes here. You will notice *Twinkle, Twinkle Little Star* appearing roughly half way through, and the main tune played on the xylophone is actually the tune from another piece by Saint-Saëns.
- Now remember the actions for the chorus section from Year 1, Lesson 11. Listen again to the complete dance. In between the first and second chorus the music sounds busy and in between the second and third chorus the music is smooth and swaying. Devise your own actions for these two sections. Base your choice of movement for the first section on busy movements such as the repeated action for a household job, and base your choice for the second section on swaying movements. The children should work out the choreography. As long as it fits the metre and the style of the music, that's fine.

Singing: *What Annie McRae Wanted For Tea* (p.86)

- Finish with a complete sing-through of this song (track 41).

Lesson 34

Objective:

- To consolidate and extend understanding of the pitched notes DO, MI and SO
- To learn a new pitch – High DO

A new pitch note – High DO

- Start with the introduction of High DO. The hand signal for this note is exactly the same as for ordinary DO, but make the fist higher. Play C on the xylophone for DO, E for MI, G for SO and then the C above that for High DO.
- Use the CD, track 42, which gives examples for the children to copy. Each example comprises three sung and played notes. When the children copy they should sing the note and also show the hand signal each time.

Singing: *Technology Grind* (music: p.88)

- With the help of the CD, track 43, start to learn *Technology Grind*. The photocopiable song sheet is at the back of the book.

Listening: 'The Swan' from *Carnival of the Animals*

- Listen to 'The Swan'. This piece is written for the cello and two pianos. The pianos represent the rippling surface of the lake, and the cello is the graceful swan gliding across the water.

Rhythm building team game in 3-time

- Finish with this team game from the last lesson, where teams of six represent two bars in 3-time.

Lesson 35

Objectives:

- To develop the skill of recognising pitched notes
- Further consolidation of stepping and clapping a metre

The pitch game

- Using the CD, track 44, play the **pitch game** now incorporating High DO with DO, MI and SO. If the children think the music ends on High DO, they should stay in the centre and put their hands on their heads.
- There are five short examples on the track, each ending on one of the four pitches. You will need to press pause in between each one. The answers and CD timings are below:
  1. DO
  2. SO   (0.12)
  3. MI   (0.24)
  4. High DO   (0.37)
  5. SO   (0.51)

Singing: *Technology Grind* (p.88)

- With the help of the the CD, track 43, revise verse one of *Technology Grind* and learn verse two.

Stepping and clapping the metre

- Track 45 provides new examples to work on.

Listening: 'The Grand Finale' of *Carnival of the Animals*

- Listen to 'The Grand Finale'. How many of the animals can the children recognise in the music? It is as though they have all come back for a bow!

Lesson 36

Objective:
- Consolidation

An activity of your choice

Singing: *Technology Grind* (p.88)
- With the help of the CD, track 43 sing *Technology Grind*. Try singing along to the accompaniment on track 46.

Sing and play any song
- Choose any song from Year 2 and create a percussion accompaniment for it.

The pitch game
- Using the CD, track 47, play the **pitch game**. There are five extracts on this track. See below for the answers:
  1. MI
  2. DO   (0.19)
  3. High DO   (0.32)
  4. SO   (0.50)
  5. SO   (1.04)

And finally!
- Finish with your favourite activity.

The Grand Old Duke Of York

Jump!

Words and music by Ann Bryant

TRACK 1 — Vocal
TRACK 2 — Backing

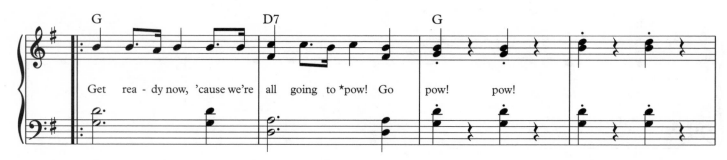

Get rea - dy now, 'cause we're all going to *pow! Go pow! pow!

Clap to the beat and you step it in a square. Yes, it's real - ly neat, so now you

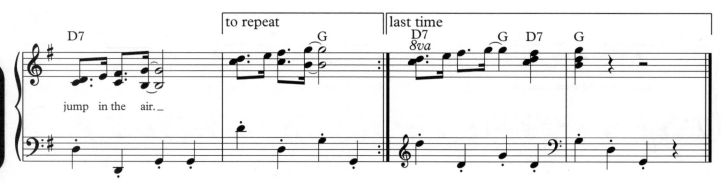

to repeat

last time

jump in the air. _

*1. pow!
2. click!
3. stamp!
4. shake!

It's me!

Words and music by Ann Bryant

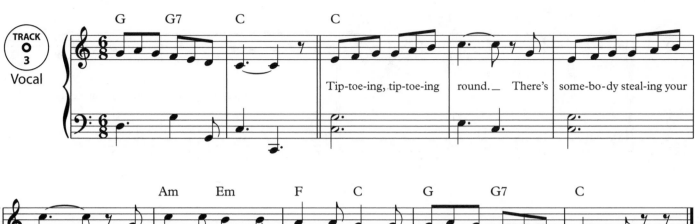

Tip-toe-ing, tip-toe-ing round.__ There's some-bo-dy steal-ing your

sound!__ Who can it be, who says 'It's me!'? The per-son who's sto-len your sound.__

The Dingleden Train

Words and music by Ann Bryant

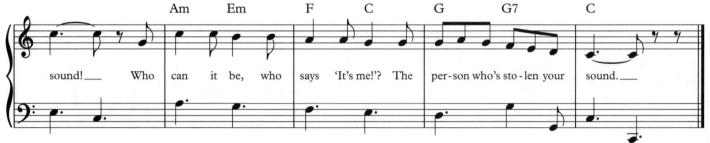

Oh the Din - gle-den Train goes

chug - ging a - long,__ chug - ging a - long,__ chug - ging a - long. Oh the

Din - gle-den Train goes chug-ging a - long,__ 'till the top meets the tip.

Remember to substitute 'Dingleden' with the name of your school
Repeat as often as necessary

Year 1 Songs

Spiller Teddy's Wellies

Words and music by Ann Bryant

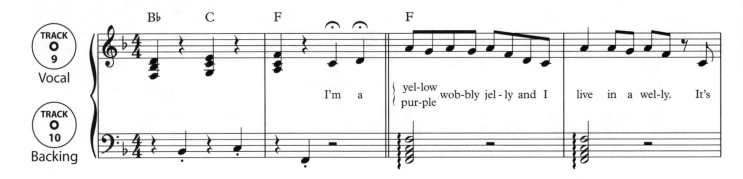

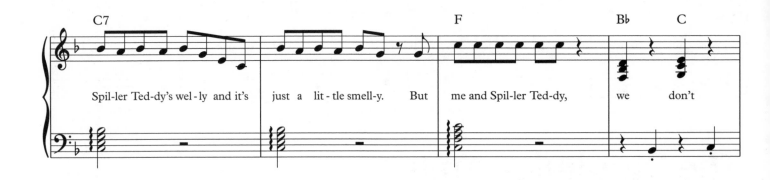

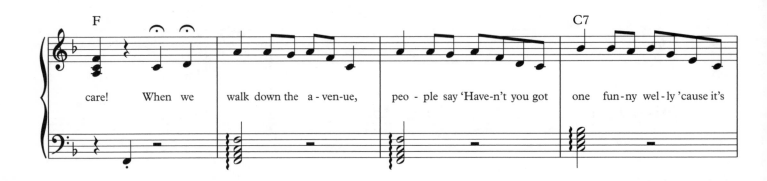

The vocal track 9 repeats back to the beginning
The backing track 10 repeats back to 'I'm a . . .'

The Hokey Cokey

Bouncily!

TRACK 11 — Vocal
TRACK 16 — Backing

*2. left arm
3. right leg
4. left leg
5. whole self

Actions:

Children should stand in a space of their own facing the teacher. The actions are the traditional ones for the first part of the song. Then follow those below for the rest of the piece:

You do the hokey cokey	*cross the arms over the chest, one arm at a time to make an 'X' and then uncross them, one arm at a time*
Turn around	*turn around once*
And that's what it's all about	*turn the palms of your hands upwards*
Oh hokey cokey cokey	*raise both arms up high, fingers reaching up to the ceiling. On the second 'cokey' do three small jumps on the spot and at the same time pull arms down in front of you, keeping the forearms vertical, with palms facing towards you to clench each fist. Repeat this for these three lines.*
And that's what it's all about	*turn the palms of your hands upwards*

This arrangement © 2001 International Music Publications Limited

Year 1 Songs

The Teeth Pop Up!

Words and music by Ann Bryant

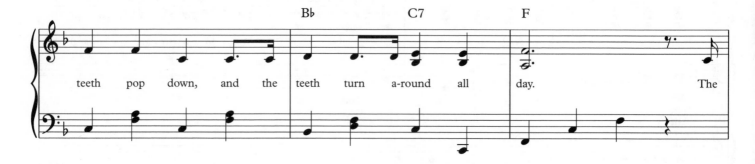

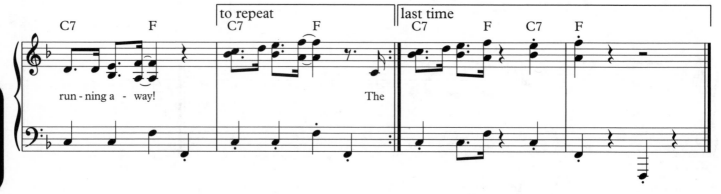

Actions:

Arrange the children in two rows (or three rows for a big class), all facing the same way.

The teeth pop up	*reach both arms up*
the teeth pop down	*crouch down and touch the ground*
turn around all day	*turn around*
getting mad	*fold the arms*
very bad	*wag one index finger as if telling someone off*
running away	*the child at the end of the row runs to join the other end*

I'm Fred Wheelie Bin

Words and music by Ann Bryant

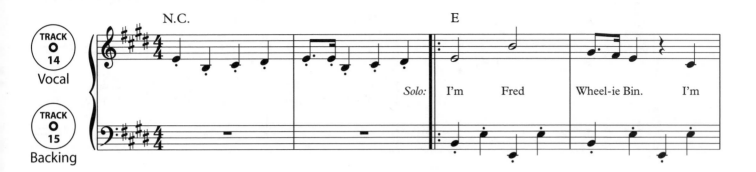

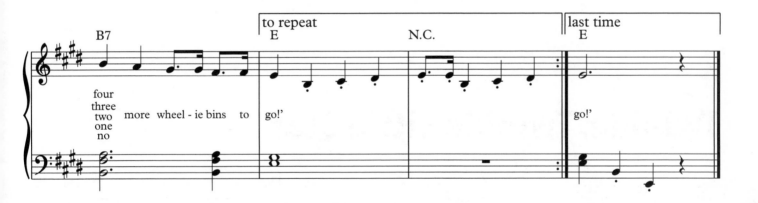

Substitute the name 'Fred' with other names of one syllable.
Choose any number of children for the row.

I Hear Thunder / Frère Jacques

New words and music by Ann Bryant

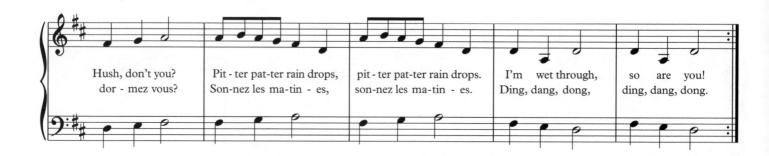

I hear thun-der, / Frè - re Jac-ques,
I hear thun-der. / Frè - re Jac-ques,
Hush, don't you? / dor - mez vous?

Hush, don't you? / dor - mez vous?
Pit - ter pat-ter rain drops, / Son-nez les ma-tin - es,
pit - ter pat-ter rain drops. / son-nez les ma-tin - es.
I'm wet through, / Ding, dang, dong,
so are you! / ding, dang, dong.

Twinkle, Twinkle Little Star

TRACK
O
30
Backing

Year 1 Songs

Hot Cross Buns / Billy Bind

New words and music by Ann Bryant

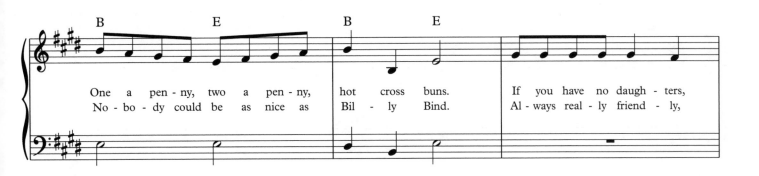

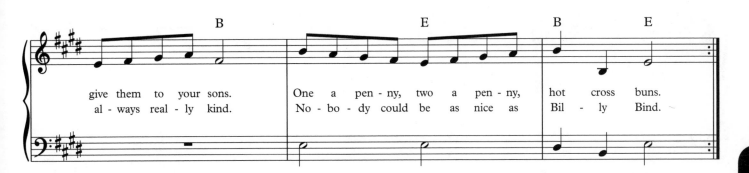

Year 1 Songs

Introducing Michael Finnigan to the Recycling Point

Words and music by Ann Bryant

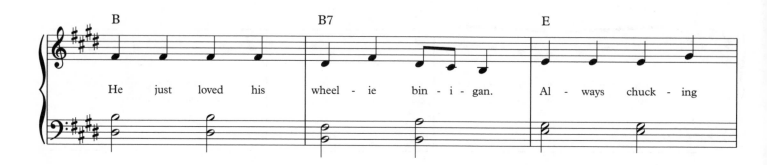

What's My Name?

Words and music by Ann Bryant

Bazookas!

Words and music by Ann Bryant

Ba - zoo-kas! I've ne - ver seen this

here be - fore!__ Ba - na - nas! I must be go - ing mad! B -

- bean-stalk, gr - grow-ing in the sk - sk - sky!__ It's big - ger than me, it's much big-ger than my

CHORUS

Dad! A bean, a bean, a bean-stalk! It's a bean, a bean, a bean-stalk! It's a

bean, a bean, a bean-stalk! I think I'll climb up, up, up, up! A bean, a bean, a bean-stalk! It's a

Year 2 Songs

bean, a bean, a bean-stalk! It's a bean, a bean, a bean-stalk! A bean, a bean, a bean-stalk!

rit.

Ba -

The Giant's Garden

Words and music by Ann Bryant

Actions:

1. No you
   can't come in
   here 'cause
   I'm
   here,
   And I'm drumming on the earth
   and I'm drumming on the walls,
   And I'm bouncing off the windows
   where the faces look so pale.
   Yes I'm drumming everywhere,
   I'm hail!

   stand with feet apart and do one stamp with the right foot
   Do one stamp with the left foot
   stretch both arms up and look up at hands
   drop arms to the sides
   crouch down and pat the floor with flat hands
   hands do 'pushing' action to the sides
   do small bounces
   stand up and run both hands over face
   turn around slowly with arms stretched out to the sides
   jump in the air and land in a shape

2. No you can't come in here 'cause I'm here,
   And I'm rattling round the house
   and I'm rattling on the roof,
   And I'm laughing at the shutters
   as they rattle back and forth.
   Yes I'm rattling like the wind
   from the North!

   as verse 1
   roll hands over and over
   roll hands over and over above heads
   do four claps
   *   with arms straight*
   turn around slowly with arms stretched out to the sides
   jump in the air and land in a shape

3. No you can't come in here 'cause I'm here,
   And I'm splintering the grass
   and I'm splintering the ground,
   And I'm writing on the windows
   with a crayon like a crack.
   Yes I'm splintering like frost,
   I'm Jack!

   as verse 1
   shake fingers
   crouch down and shake fingers
   pretend to write some pointed W's in the air,
   *   in joined up writing*
   turn around slowly with arms stretched out to the sides
   jump in the air and land in a shape

4. No you can't come in here 'cause I'm here,
   And I'm blanketing the hills,
   and I'm blanketing the trees,
   And I've taken all the warmth,
   that's why the birds have had to go.
   Yes I'm blanketing the world,
   I'm snow!

   as verse 1
   shape hands over pretend hills
   reach up and shape hands over pretend tree tops
   hug self as though cold
   flap arms like wings
   turn around slowly with arms stretched out to the sides
   jump in the air and land in a shape

5. No you can't come in here 'cause I'm here,
   I'm more deadly than the snow,
   I'm more deadly than the frost,
   I'm more deadly than the wind and hail,
   more deadly than a vice.
   Nobody can cut through me,
   Nobody can cut through me,
   I'm ice!

   as verse 1
   hug self
   crouch down and shake fingers
   quickly roll hands over and over, then do a 'pushing' action to each side
   bang floor with hands
   very slowly rise up from the floor and turn at the same time
   *   – look menacing!*
   jump in the air and land in a shape

Mum! Mum! Quickly Come

Words and music by Ann Bryant

Year 2 Songs

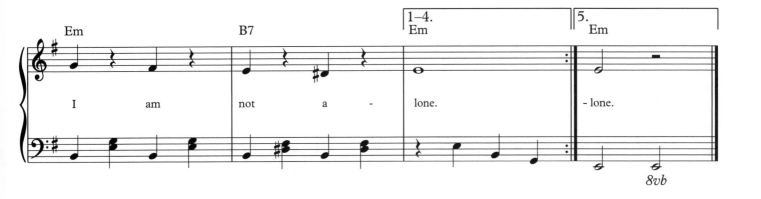

1. I saw a giant on the wall.
   It stood there fifty metres tall.
   It made me feel so very small.
   It was a giant on the wall, so I called,

   Mum! Mum! quickly come,
   I'm not staying here on my own.
   Mum! Mum! quickly come,
   Something tells me I am not alone.

2. I saw a bundle of fur in the air.
   It growled at me like a grizzly bear.
   It fixed me with its beady stare.
   You know you mustn't stare at a bear, so I called,

3. I saw a snake hanging from the light.
   It hissed at me, 'Mind the bugs don't bite!'
   My goose bumps bumped and my face went white.
   It was a snake hanging from the light, so I called,

4. I saw a bee on my pillowcase.
   It made a beeline for my face.
   It gave my heartbeat quite a race.
   It was a bee on my pillowcase, so I called,

5. I saw a mouse scuttle under my bed.
   'Eek, eek, squeak, squeak, nibble, nibble,' it said.
   'I'm only here for a piece of cheese.
   Don't tell your Mum, oh please don't, please!' So I yelled,

Rats!

Words and music by Ann Bryant

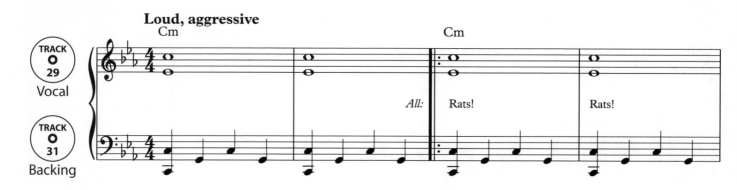

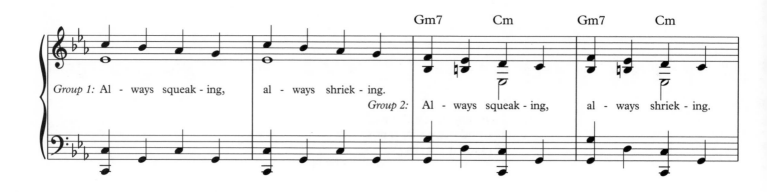

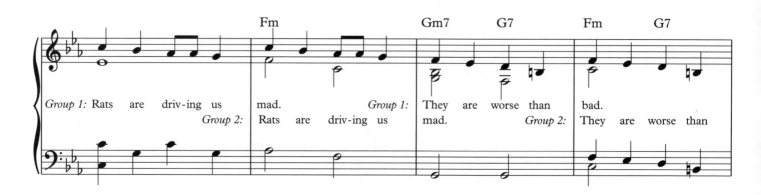

Year 2
Songs

In The Crocodile Pool

Words and music by Ann Bryant

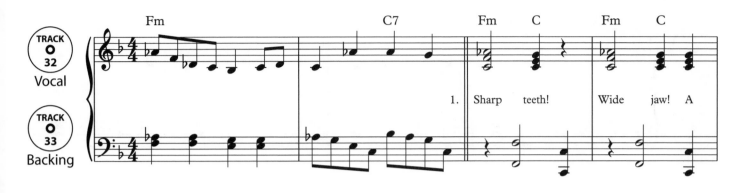

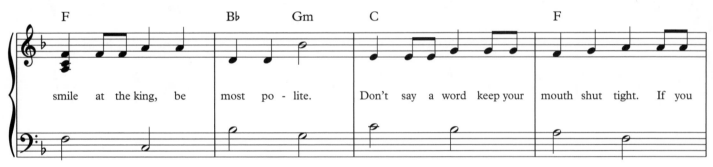

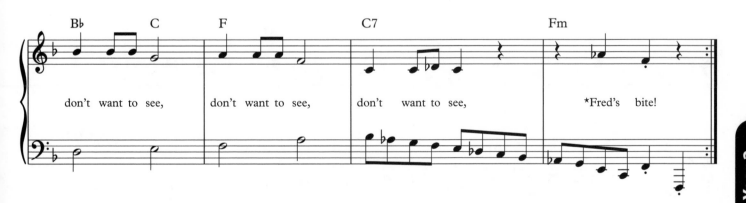

*1. Fred
2. Bill
3. Don

Year 2 Songs

I'm Sorry

Words and music by Ann Bryant

TRACK
O
35
Vocal

TRACK
O
38
Backing

1. Tom was play-ing ball one day, he kicked, he bounced, he threw it. Smash went a win-dow,

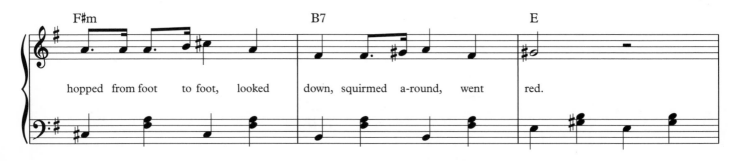

Dad blew a fuse and said, 'Tom did you do it?' Tom bit his lip and hopped from foot to foot, looked down, squirmed a-round, went red.

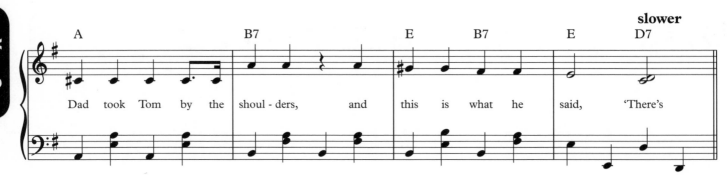

Dad took Tom by the shoul-ders, and this is what he said, 'There's

Year 2 Songs

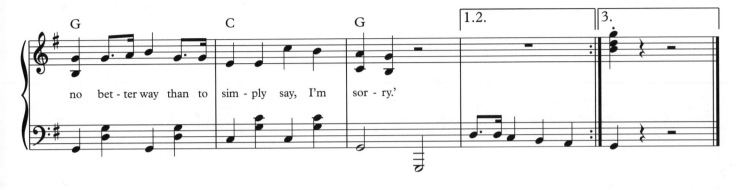

1. Tom was playing ball one day,
   He kicked, he bounced, he threw it.
   Smash went a window,
   Dad blew a fuse and said, 'Tom did you do it?'
   Tom bit his lip and hopped from foot to foot,
   Looked down, squirmed around, went red.
   Dad took Tom by the shoulders,
   And this is what he said,

   'There's no better way than to simply say, I'm sorry.
   Got that?
   There's no better way than to simply say, I'm sorry.'

2. Lizzie broke a vase one day,
   And wondered could she glue it?
   She patched it up but Mum saw the crack,
   And said, 'Liz, did you do it?'
   Liz bit her lip and hopped from foot to foot,
   Looked down, squirmed around, went red.
   Mum took Liz by the shoulders,
   And this is what she said,

3. Ben ate a block of Granny's chocolate,
   Far too fast to chew it.
   Gran, feeling peckish, couldn't find the chocolate,
   Said, 'Ben, did you do it?'
   Ben bit his lip and hopped from foot to foot,
   Looked down, squirmed around, went red.
   Gran took Ben by the shoulders,
   And this is what she said,

Year 2
Songs

85

What Annie McRae Wanted For Tea

Words and music by Ann Bryant

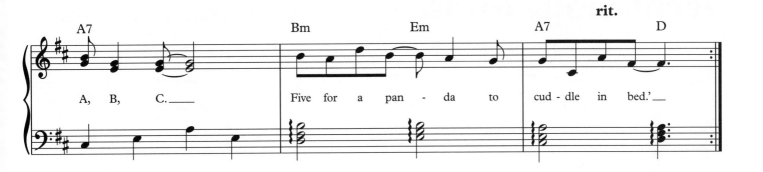

1. At five years old Annie McRae had chips for tea every day.
    So when it was teatime her mother would say,
    'How many chips do you want today?'

    Said Annie, 'One for a garden full of pansies for me,
    Two for my cat and three for Big Ted!
    Four not to have to learn my A, B, C.
    Five for a panda to cuddle in bed.'

2. At six years old Annie McRae had pancakes for tea every day.
    So when it was teatime her mother would say,
    'How many pancakes do you want today?'

    Said Annie, 'One for a video of Winnie the Pooh,
    Two for ice cream and three lots of snow.
    Four for a midnight feast with Lizzie and Sue.
    Five to have hair that could magically grow.'

3. At seven years old Annie McRae had cherries for tea every day.
    So when it was teatime her mother would say,
    'How many cherries do you want today?'

    Said Annie, 'One for my family and all of my friends,
    Two to be kind and three to be true.
    Four to be healthy and to never tell lies.
    Five you love me and six I love you.'

Technology Grind

Words and music by Ann Bryant

Fast and frantic

TRACK 43 — Vocal
TRACK 46 — Backing

1. Or - gan - i - sa - tion, the

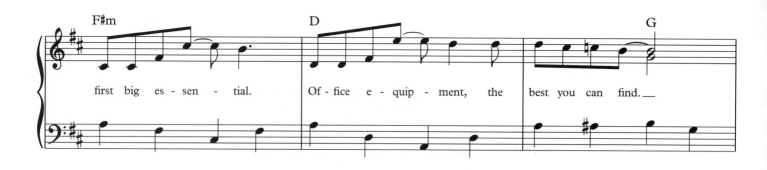

first big es - sen - tial. Of - fice e - quip - ment, the best you can find.__

En - ter com - mu - ters, work on com - pu - ters. Day af - ter day the tech -

slower and calmer

-no - lo - gy grind.__ But I pre - fer to work in my gar - den, to

work in my gar - den at home. I have all that I need__ right here in my gar - den. I'm

1. Organisation, the first big essential.
Office equipment, the best you can find.
Enter commuters, work on computers.
Day after day the technology grind.

   But I prefer to work in my garden,
   To work in my garden at home.
   I have all that I need
   Right here in my garden.
   I'm living the life that I've grown.

2. Order the software and order the hardware.
Paper and printout the best of its kind.
Enter commuters, work on computers.
Day after day the technology grind.

3. Te-li-comm-uni-ca-pho-ni-ca-dict-o
Da-ta-per-dig-i-tal-au-to-re-wind!
Enter commuters, work on computers.
Day after day the technology grind.

   The first two lines of verse 3 are a mixture of
   real technology words and made-up jargon!

Year 2 Songs

What's My Name?   by Ann Bryant

1. Is it John? Is it Don?
   Is it David, Danny, Dick?
   Peter or Paul?
   Is it Reginald or Rick?
   Bob? Is it Job? Is it Robby, Nobby, Nick?
   Oh what, what, what could it be?

   (Rumplestiltskin)
   Hee, hee, hee, hee
   Ho, Ho, Ho!
   What my name is, you don't know.
   Hee, hee, hee, hee
   Ho, Ho, Ho!
   Nobody knows it,
   Oh no!

2. Is it Tim? Is it Tom?
   Is it Leslie, Laurie, Len?
   Harry, Larry, Gary?
   Or is it Bill or Ben?
   Flute? Boot? Rooty- tooty- toot?
   Oh what, what, what could it be?

   Chorus

3. Is it Ming? Is it Wing? Is it Ting-a-ling-a-ling?
   Ping-pong? Sing-song? Ding Dang Dong?
   Rip-rap? Snip-snap? Polly-wolly doodle?
   Oh what, what, what could it be?

   Chorus

Year 2 Songsheets

Bazookas!   by Ann Bryant

Bazookas!
I've never seen this here before!
Bananas!
I must be going mad!
B-beanstalk, gr-growing in the sk-sk-sky!
It's bigger than me, it's much bigger than my Dad!

A bean, a bean, a beanstalk!
It's a bean, a bean, a beanstalk!
It's a bean, a bean, a beanstalk!
I think I'll climb up, up, up, up!
A bean, a bean, a beanstalk!
It's a bean, a bean, a beanstalk!
It's a bean, a bean, a beanstalk!
A bean, a bean, a beanstalk!

Year 2 Songsheets

The Giant's Garden   by Ann Bryant

1. No you can't come in here 'cause I'm here,
   And I'm drumming on the earth and I'm drumming on the walls,
   And I'm bouncing off the windows where the faces look so pale.
   Yes I'm drumming everywhere, I'm hail!

2. No you can't come in here 'cause I'm here,
   And I'm rattling round the house and I'm rattling on the roof,
   And I'm laughing at the shutters as they rattle back and forth.
   Yes I'm rattling like the wind from the North!

3. No you can't come in here 'cause I'm here,
   And I'm splintering the grass and I'm splintering the ground,
   And I'm writing on the windows with a crayon like a crack.
   Yes I'm splintering like frost, I'm Jack!

4. No you can't come in here 'cause I'm here,
   And I'm blanketing the hills, and I'm blanketing the trees,
   And I've taken all the warmth, that's why the birds have had to go.
   Yes I'm blanketing the world, I'm snow!

5. No you can't come in here 'cause I'm here,
   I'm more deadly than the snow, I'm more deadly than the frost,
   I'm more deadly than the wind and hail, more deadly than a vice.
   Nobody can cut through me,
   Nobody can cut through me, I'm ice!

Year 2
Songsheets

Mum! Mum! Quickly Come   by Ann Bryant

1. I saw a giant on the wall.
   It stood there fifty metres tall.
   It made me feel so very small.
   It was a giant on the wall, so I called,

   Mum! Mum! quickly come,
   I'm not staying here on my own.
   Mum! Mum! quickly come,
   Something tells me I am not alone.

2. I saw a bundle of fur in the air.
   It growled at me like a grizzly bear.
   It fixed me with its beady stare.
   You know you mustn't stare at a bear, so I called,

   Chorus

3. I saw a snake hanging from the light.
   It hissed at me, 'Mind the bugs don't bite!'
   My goose bumps bumped and my face went white.
   It was a snake hanging from the light, so I called,

   Chorus

4. I saw a bee on my pillowcase.
   It made a beeline for my face.
   It gave my heartbeat quite a race.
   It was a bee on my pillowcase, so I called,

   Chorus

5. I saw a mouse scuttle under my bed.
   'Eek, eek, squeak, squeak, nibble, nibble,' it said.
   'I'm only here for a piece of cheese.
   Don't tell your Mum, oh please don't, please!'
   So I yelled,

   Chorus

Year 2 Songsheets

Rats!   by Ann Bryant

Group 1

1. Rats! Rats!
   Always squeaking, always shrieking.
   Rats are driving us mad.
   They are worse than bad.
   They're disgusting!

2. Rats! Rats!
   Always squeaking, always shrieking.
   Rats are driving us mad.
   They are worse than bad.
   They're revolting!

Group 2

1. Rats! Rats!
   Always squeaking, always shrieking.
   Rats are driving us mad.
   They are worse than bad.
   They're disgusting!

2. Rats! Rats!
   Always squeaking, always shrieking.
   Rats are driving us mad.
   They are worse than bad.
   They're revolting!

Year 2 Songsheets

In the Crocodile Pool   by Ann Bryant

1. Sharp teeth!
   Wide jaw!
   A gleam in the eye like you never saw before.
   It's a crocodile, ★Fred!
   In the crocodile pool.

   So smile at the king, be most polite.
   Don't say a word keep your mouth shut tight.
   If you don't want to see, don't want to see,
   Don't want to see,
   ★Fred's bite!

2. ★Bill

3. ★Don

Year 2 Songsheets

I'm Sorry   by Ann Bryant

1. Tom was playing ball one day,
   He kicked, he bounced, he threw it.
   Smash went a window,
   Dad blew a fuse and said, 'Tom did you do it?'
   Tom bit his lip and hopped from foot to foot,
   Looked down, squirmed around, went red.
   Dad took Tom by the shoulders,
   And this is what he said,

   'There's no better way than to simply say, I'm sorry.
   Got that?
   There's no better way than to simply say, I'm sorry.'

2. Lizzie broke a vase one day,
   And wondered could she glue it?
   She patched it up but Mum saw the crack,
   And said, 'Liz, did you do it?'
   Liz bit her lip and hopped from foot to foot,
   Looked down, squirmed around, went red.
   Mum took Liz by the shoulders,
   And this is what she said,

   Chorus

3. Ben ate a block of Granny's chocolate,
   Far too fast to chew it.
   Gran, feeling peckish, couldn't find the chocolate,
   Said, 'Ben, did you do it?'
   Ben bit his lip and hopped from foot to foot,
   Looked down, squirmed around, went red.
   Gran took Ben by the shoulders,
   And this is what she said,

   Chorus

Year 2
Songsheets

What Annie McRae Wanted For Tea   by Ann Bryant

1. At five years old Annie McRae had chips for tea every day.
    So when it was teatime her mother would say,
    'How many chips do you want today?'

    Said Annie, 'One for a garden full of pansies for me,
    Two for my cat and three for Big Ted!
    Four not to have to learn my A, B, C.
    Five for a panda to cuddle in bed.'

2. At six years old Annie McRae had pancakes for tea every day.
    So when it was teatime her mother would say,
    'How many pancakes do you want today?'

    Said Annie, 'One for a video of Winnie the Pooh,
    Two for ice cream and three lots of snow.
    Four for a midnight feast with Lizzie and Sue.
    Five to have hair that could magically grow.'

3. At seven years old Annie McRae had cherries for tea every day.
    So when it was teatime her mother would say,
    'How many cherries do you want today?'

    Said Annie, 'One for my family and all of my friends,
    Two to be kind and three to be true.
    Four to be healthy and to never tell lies.
    Five you love me and six I love you.'

Year 2 Songsheets

Technology Grind

by Ann Bryant

1. Organisation, the first big essential.
   Office equipment, the best you can find.
   Enter commuters, work on computers.
   Day after day the technology grind.

   But I prefer to work in my garden,
   To work in my garden at home.
   I have all that I need
   Right here in my garden.
   I'm living the life that I've grown.

2. Order the software and order the hardware.
   Paper and printout the best of its kind.
   Enter commuters, work on computers.
   Day after day the technology grind.

   Chorus

3. Te-li-comm-uni-ca-pho-ni-ca-dict-o
   Data-per-dig-i-tal-au-to-re-wind!
   Enter commuters, work on computers.
   Day after day the technology grind.

   Chorus

Year 2 Songsheets

Appendices

The National Curriculum for England Key Stage 1 – Music

Contrast cards (photocopiable)
Note value cards (photocopiable)

Photocopy these and divide up into individual cards. Back them with strong card for durability.

Assessment Grid (photocopiable)

This is my recommended sample assessment grid to help you keep a continuous assessment of your children with the minimum amount of paperwork.

Name only those children who are under-achieving or over-achieving. Whenever you think there has been a good opportunity in a lesson to assess any of the given objectives, fill in the appropriate part of the grid.

By using this user-friendly grid you can simply assume that those children not named are achieving satisfactorily. You might choose to complete several grids over the two years.

Activities and where they are first taught

CD track listing

National Curriculum for England Key Stage 1 – Music

During Key Stage 1 pupils listen carefully and respond physically to a wide range of music. They play musical instruments and sing a variety of songs from memory, adding accompaniments and creating short compositions, with increasing confidence, imagination and control. They explore and enjoy how sounds and silence can create different moods and effects.

Knowledge, skills and understanding

Teaching should ensure that **listening**, and **applying knowledge and understanding**, are developed through the interrelated skills of **performing**, **composing** and **appraising**.

Controlling sounds through singing and playing – performing skills
1.   Pupils should be taught how to:
    a) use their voices expressively by singing songs and speaking chants and rhymes
    b) play tuned and untuned instruments
    c) rehearse and perform with others (for example starting and finishing together, keeping to a steady pulse)

Creating and developing musical ideas – composing skills
2.   Pupils should be taught how to:
    a) create musical patterns
    b) explore, choose and organise sounds and musical ideas

Responding and reviewing – appraising skills
3.   Pupils should be taught how to:
    a) explore and express their ideas and feelings about music using movement, dance and expressive musical language
    b) make improvements to their own work

Listening, and applying knowledge and understanding
4.   Pupils should be taught:
    a) to listen with concentration and to internalise and recall sounds with increasing aural memory
    b) how the combined musical elements of pitch, duration, dynamics, tempo, timbre, texture and silence can be organised and used expressively within simple structures (for example, beginning, middle, end)
    c) how sounds can be made in different ways (for example, vocalising, clapping, by musical instruments, in the environment) and described using given and invented signs and symbols
    d) how music is used for particular purposes (for example for dance, as a lullaby)

Breadth of study

5.   During the key stage pupils should be taught the **Knowledge, skills and understanding** through:
    a) a range of musical activities that integrate performing, composing and appraising
    b) respond to a range of musical and non-musical starting points
    c) working on their own, in groups of different sizes and as a class
    d) a range of live and recorded music from different times and cultures

Contrast cards

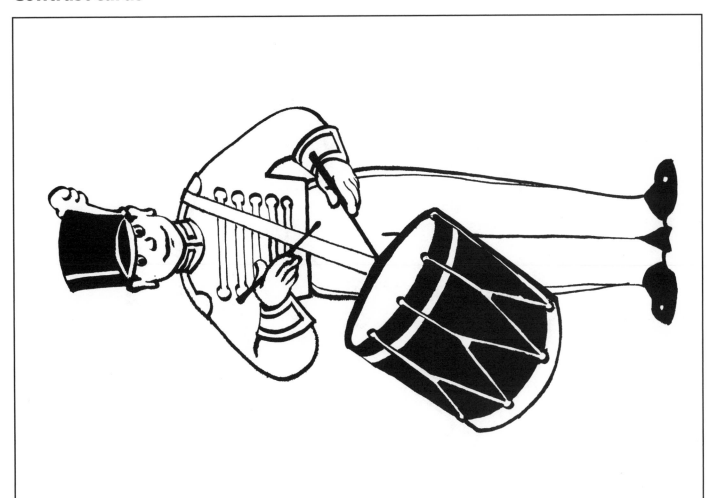

Contrast cards

Contrast cards

Contrast cards

Note value cards

Note value cards

106

Assessment Grid

Objectives	Date	Under-achieving	Over-achieving
1. Ability to focus (looking, listening and concentrating) e.g. when playing the **Contrasts** game			
2. Ability to sustain concentration e.g. when listening to *Carnival of the Animals*			
3. Ability to discriminate aurally e.g. **Equal claps around the circle**			
4. Ability to respond quickly and accurately e.g. **Signals**			
5. Rhythmic awareness e.g. **Clapping note values**			
6. Understanding of rhythmic notation e.g. **Magic cards**			
7. Ability to sing (Take into consideration participation, confidence, tunefulness, expressive quality, performance quality.)			
8. Ability to play percussion instruments (Take into consideration all of the above points from no. 7 plus coordination and technique)			
9. Ability to be self-critical in order to improve general musicianship			
10. Pitch awareness (n/a in Year 1) e.g. **Copying three sounds with voice and hand signals**			

Activities and where they are first taught

YEAR 1, TERM 1

Contrasts	Lesson 2
Signals	Lesson 2
Pass the contrasts cards	Lesson 3
Signals (the elimination game)	Lesson 4
Equal claps around the circle	Lesson 10

YEAR 1, TERM 2

Pass the notes round the circle	Lesson 13
Stepping and clapping note values	Lesson 13
Stepping note values in groups	Lesson 14
Playing note values in groups	Lesson 15
Magic cards	Lesson 17
Follow the conductor	Lesson 23

YEAR 1, TERM 3

Extended stepping and clapping note values	Lesson 25
Responding to food rhythms in groups	Lesson 29
Find Michael Finnigan!	Lesson 31
Extended magic cards	Lesson 33
If it's your name, run!	Lesson 33
Extended magic cards 2	Lesson 35

YEAR 2, TERM 1

Stepping a sequence	Lesson 1
Singing and growing	Lesson 1
Copying three sounds with voice and hand signals	Lesson 2
Guess the food rhythms	Lesson 3
Clapping back food rhythms	Lesson 5
The pitch game	Lesson 7

YEAR 2, TERM 2

8, 4, 2 activity	Lesson 13
Extended magic cards 3	Lesson 15
The code game	Lesson 16
Clapping on different beats	Lesson 17
Canon	Lesson 19

YEAR 2, TERM 3

Stepping and stopping	Lesson 25
Random contrasts cards	Lesson 25
Stepping and clapping the metre	Lesson 30
Collecting animal noises	Lesson 31
Collecting note values	Lesson 31

CD Track Listing

Year 1

1. Jump! (vocal)
2. Jump! (backing)
3. It's Me!
4. The Dingleden Train
5. Mummies' notes (crotchets)
6. Great-Grandads' notes (minims)
7. Children's notes (quavers)
8. Mixing up of crotchets, minims and quavers
9. Spiller Teddy's Wellies (vocal)
10. Spiller Teddy's Wellies (backing: 11 play-throughs)
11. The Hokey Cokey (vocal)
12. The Teeth Pop Up! (vocal)
13. The Teeth Pop Up! (backing: 6 play-throughs)
14. I'm Fred Wheelie Bin (vocal)
15. I'm Fred Wheelie Bin (backing)
16. The Hokey Cokey (backing)
17. Introducing Michael Finnigan to the Recycling Point (vocal)
18. Introducing Michael Finnigan to the Recycling Point (backing)

Year 2

19. What's My Name? (vocal)
20. What's My Name? (backing)
21. Bazookas! (vocal)
22. Bazookas! (backing)
23. The food rhythms
24. The Giant's Garden (vocal)
25. The Giant's Garden (backing)
26. Music for the 8, 4, 2 activity
27. Mum! Mum! Quickly Come (vocal)
28. Mum! Mum! Quickly Come (backing)
29. Rats! (vocal)
30. Twinkle, Twinkle Little Star (backing)
31. Rats! (backing)
32. In the Crocodile Pool (vocal)
33. In the Crocodile Pool (backing)
34. Random contrasts cards
35. I'm Sorry (vocal)
36. Rhythm building without food words
37. Random contrasts cards
38. I'm Sorry (backing)
39. What Annie McCrae Wanted For Tea (vocal)
40. Stepping and clapping the metre 1
41. What Annie McCrae Wanted For Tea (backing)
42. Do, Mi, So, High Do examples
43. Technology Grind (vocal)
44. The pitch game 1
45. Stepping and clapping the metre 2
46. Technology Grind (backing)
47. The pitch game 2

2/04